YOU CAN
MAKE A
determined
DIFFERENCE

...in an environment of COMPETITIVENESS

– A must read for anyone seeking leadership role –

by
SOLOMON B. BABAJIDE

Thanks for always making the DETERMINED difference!

Jan. 30, 2016

INTRODUCTION

YOU ONLY LIVE ONCE...

*H*ave you determined what you want out of life? Do you know what you are living for and are passionate about? Do you know what you are **committed to** as opposed to what your life's mandate is?

Do you know what gift God has deposited in/bestowed on you; with which you are to fulfill your God-given call?

Has it ever occurred to you that...

"By faith Moses, when he was come to years, refused to be called the son of Pharaoh's daughter; **Choosing rather to suffer affliction with the people of God**, than to enjoy the pleasures of sin for a season; Esteeming the reproach of Christ greater riches than the treasures in Egypt: for he had respect unto the recompense of the reward. By faith he forsook Egypt, not fearing the wrath of the king: for he endured, as seeing him who is invisible."–Hebrews 11:24-27 [KJV]

It is incumbent on each Christian to discover what God's predetermined purpose and calling are for their lives and to begin to operate in the realm of their existence.

In the words of Bill Watterson[1]:

> "We all have different desires and needs, but if we don't discover what we want from ourselves and what we stand for, we will live passively and unfulfilled."

In Judges 9:7-15, we understand that the trees know why they were created. We also know from the Scriptures that the cattle on thousand hills, the birds of the air and the fishes in the sea are all created to honor God – Isaiah 43 and to bless mankind.

> I'm not stubborn,
> I'm just REALLY
> determined.

----

[1] Bill Watterson [b.1957]: https://en.wikipedia.org/wiki/Bill_Watterson

ACKNOWLEDGEMENT

This is simply my story, presented as a prose.

It tells my humble beginning as an office clerk, rising through the ranks to the position of Group Coordinator of a Fortune 500.

A number of professional and spiritual personalities contributed in no small measure to my success among whom were Seaboard Corporation's Harry Bresky, Steve Bresky, Robert I. Fleming and Joe Rodrigues. Arch-Bishop Benson Idahosa of the Church of God Mission was a rare mentor. Even though some of these may no longer be around, their guidance particularly in those challenging situations will never be forgotten.

I wholeheartedly appreciate the encouragement and support of my wife and children in ensuring that this project becomes a reality.

BIBLE QUOTATIONS

All Scripture references used in this Book have been taken from multiple versions of the Bible Hub Online Parallel Bible Study in order to provide clarity and related expression of the topics covered. In particular, the following versions have particular relevance to the work:

KJV – King James Version: Copyright © 2012; BibleProtector.com; INT Bible. Used by Permission

BLB – Berean Literal Bible: Copyright © 2015 by Bible Hub and BereanBible.com. Used by Permission

AKJV – American King James Version & KJVA–King James Version, American Edition: Produced by Stone Engelbrite; Courtesy BereanBible.com; Copyright © 1999, 2013, 2014 Used by Permission

ESV – English Standard Version: Copyright © 2001 by Crossway Bibles; Publishing ministry of Good News Publishers

NASB – New American Standard Bible: Copyright © 1960–1995 by The Lockman Foundation

NIV – New International Version: Copyright © 1973, 1978, 1984, 2011 by Biblica®

GWT – God's Word Translation: Copyright work of God's Word to the Nations. 1995

NLT – New Living Translation: Copyright ©1996, 2004, 2007. Used by permission of Tyndale House Publishers, Inc., Carol Stream, Illinois 60188

TABLE OF CONTENT

PREFACE
MAKE A Determined DIFFERENCE

*I*t is increasingly becoming more and more of a challenge to find exemplary and sustainable leadership, thanks to today's "get to the top by whatever means" mindset. In today's market place it is an easy, rather common parlance, to suppose that the end justifies the means – whatever that means to realize achievement may be.

It used to be that men and women were content to hear the traditional "rags to riches" stories and were motivated to emulate those character TRAITS that enabled the story-teller succeed. That seems to be in the past. We seem to now be in the era of "get it while it lasts" and "the patient dog ends up getting the leanest bone."

We have moved from the doctrine of the diligent to the company of "the smartest gets it all" thereby rendering the reward for excellence and the essence of the *Race To The Top*[1] policy meaningless.

Traditional values with the emphasis on doing it right have been spurned and corner-cutting embraced.

Worse still is the fact that in the face of today's multifaceted paths and pulls, it takes extra-ordinary efforts to focus, discover and proceed in the right direction. It takes more than mere attention to sieve today's fast-paced, high-tech realities from look-alikes. It takes keenness and without any doubt, it takes unrelenting desire and deliberate choice to make a "**determined**" difference.

Making a difference doesn't come easy on either side of life's continuum. While we're on this side of the divide, there continues to be a price to making a difference–positively or negatively. Notoriety and failure have their price. So also do fame, prestige and success. Most people desire to make positive difference but with negative, out-of-date, unrealistic and ill-prepared approaches. Others choose to do nothing and are rewarded by deserving outcome.

Down the ages, people that have made positive impact have always applied principles that made them stand out among many their equals.

The principles that I am sharing in this book will apply to the religious, the faithful as well as the indifferent.

In the religious circles, the Bible stories provide ample evidences of men and women that chose to make determined difference by exemplary lifestyles. By their successes, they have gained entry into the Book of Life – some in little, minor ways while others received glowing tributes that could be regarded as major. But all of them without exception embraced some or all of the principles that are contained in this book.

Jacob's story was quite unique. His birth, his childhood, his marriage, his working life, his travels, all told of a man that chose to make a DETERMINED difference. He was quick to spot opportunities – Genesis 25:19-34. He was spiritually sensitive as he made contact with heaven and the beckoning angels ascending and descending – Genesis 28:11-17. At other times, he wrestled with the visiting angel who would bless him and change his name permanently for posterity – Genesis 32:24-30. This is a man who would not be deterred by a would-be father-in-law that changed his marriage contractual terms, making him serve twice the years agreed – Genesis 29:21-30; as well as his wages – ten times!–Genesis 31:6-7, 41. But for his determination to make a difference, Jacob would have succumbed to the pressure of blackmail and betrayal. He did not.

Joseph made a DETERMINED difference in his prison-to-palace experience–Genesis 37, 39, 40, 41.

He was envied. He was planned against. He was dropped in the pit to die. His brethren reported him as dead to his parent. He was sold as slave. He suffered servitude in the house of Pharaoh's Captain Portiphah. He was falsely accused and imprisoned. And when he helped those that he thought were in position to put in good word for him before the king, was abandoned and forgotten. Yet in all of these, his faith was fixed. His determination was unwavering nor will he compromise his FAITH and INTEGRITY. It did not take long before his resolve was rewarded. He became the Prime Minister in the land–next only to King Pharaoh himself.

Moses also made a DETERMINED difference...

He chose rather to suffer the afflictions that confronted him than the momentary pleasures and fame of Pharaoh's palace – Hebrews 11:25. He identified with his people that were despised in slavery [- Exodus 2-6]. He was willing and ready to pay the price for the fulfillment of the glory that lied ahead of him and his people. He sensed that to not do so was to travel the path of forfeiture of eternal destiny.

David made a DETERMINED difference...

Each time that he faced the tricks and antics of Saul, and the test of his faith, he behaved himself wisely... remembering the promises of God about him. In the face of covenant relationship with Saul's son–Jonathan, the Scriptures say about David, *"he behaved himself wisely"* [v.5]. When King Saul promoted him military captain cum aide-camp, perhaps in order to have him close enough and be available for his nefarious intention, we also read that David *"behaved himself wisely in all his ways"*–v. 14. And when these did not work in getting at David, Saul chose the open enmity route. Yet David would not let his guard down but *"behaved himself more wisely..."*–v. 30. He chose to make the determined difference.

Prophet Samuel made a DETERMINED difference... He was a man that lived in integrity. Hear what he challenged Israel with:

"... Behold, I have hearkened unto your voice in all that ye said unto me, and have made a king over you. And now, behold, the king walketh before you: and I am old and gray-headed; and, behold, my sons are with you: and I have walked before you from my childhood unto this day. Behold, here I am: witness against me before the LORD, and before his anointed: whose ox have I taken? or whose ass have I taken? or whom have I defrauded? whom have I oppressed? or of whose hand have I received any bribe to blind mine eyes therewith? and I will restore it you. And they said, Thou hast not defrauded us, nor oppressed us, neither hast thou taken ought of any man's hand. And he said unto them, The LORD is witness against you, and his anointed is witness this day, that ye have not found ought in my hand. And they answered, He is witness."
- I Samuel 12:1-5 [KJV]

Deborah, Israel's only female Judge was a prophetess and distinguished wife! She made a DETERMINED difference among the women of her days – Judges 4 & 5. So did Daniel, Shadrach, Meshach and Abednego – Daniel 3. These defied the lions and fiery furnaces. Read Hebrews 11 and the list is endless, of those who by faith chose to make a DETERMINED difference!

And in the New Testament, the disciples and apostles – both those who were with Jesus and those that came after His earthly appearance were people that deliberately chose to make a DIFFERENCE.

And Jesus? He made a remarkable, DETERMINED difference. Being God the Son, He endured the cross and despised shame as He looked forward to the fulfillment of the glory that was ahead.

We read in Hebrews 12:2:

"Looking unto Jesus... who for the joy that was set before Him endured the cross, despising the shame, and is set down at the right hand of the throne of God..." [KJV]

"When He was reviled, He did not retaliate and when He suffered, He did not threaten..."–I Peter 2:23 [BLB]

"And though He were a Son, He learned obedience by the things He suffered... and became the Author of eternal salvation"–Hebrews 5:8-9 [KJVA]

The principles applied by the religious worthies were not religiously exclusive. In our modern world, there have been numerous outstanding men and women that made DETERMINED difference as they changed their communities and the world at large:

Steve Jobs [1955–2011] was one of them. From educational obscurity, he went ahead to found what was to transform the computer age in what became Apple Computers. That was nothing short of making a DETERMINED difference.

South Africa's Nelson Mandela [1918-2013] spent 20 years in jail only to come out and become the President of his country. By standing against apartheid, the nation's rulers could not resist the determination of this larger-than-life man to see freedom and human dignity evolve!

Oprah Winfrey [1954 to-date], America's talk show host, is supposedly the richest and the most influential woman in the U.S. She is a passionate believer in self-improvement and works hard to make a DETERMINED difference.

Russia's Mikhail Gorbachev [1931 to-date], against all odds and threats to his life, had the courage and strength of character to confront age-old Soviet Communism and to move the Union to democracy and respect for human rights. That was a testimony to the power of making a DETERMINED difference.

Erstwhile and only woman British Prime Minister Margaret Thatcher [1925–2013], ruled Britain for over a decade and changed the landscape of British politics for good. She emphasized individual responsibility to leadership and was called the "Iron Lady" of Britain by her strong will and determination to make the difference.

Here at home, the name Barak Obama [1961 to-date] will go down the world's history as the first black man to become America's two-time President. By defying racial and class barriers that has kept many black people away from such leadership role, Mr. Obama steadily but surely made significant and DETERMINED difference.

There are countless others – living and dead: Microsoft's Bill Gates, Human Rights activist Martin Luther King, Mother Theresa, Poland's Lech Walesa, American President Bill Clinton, India's Prime Minister Indira Gandhi, and many more. There are yet others – prominent "Rags-To-Riches" celebrities who against all odds made significant successful and enduring impact to their world. They were thought to have been dealt lemon but turned it to pleasurable lemonade!

A business friend recently told me how his dad, a Polish immigrant came into the United States several years back – with nothing to his name. He went to the elementary school and high school. Upon graduation, he was hired by a little known company then as a sales person. Determined to make a difference and in conjunction with the efforts of his other salesmen, the company's product began to make profitable in-road into the American market. But my friend's dad out-performed his other colleagues, becoming the best salesman of the year many times over. Taking advantage of the opportunity to buy the company – when it became available, my dad's friend went ahead to own a company whose product has since become a household name. The rest of that story has become history.

There are undoubtedly exceptional others who have success stories that inspire. From the likes of President Barak Obama who in spite of the fact that his immigrant father was not in his life and from a humble beginning went ahead and through determination applied the principles of making the difference and rose above his equals, to becoming one of the world's most prominent, to the likes of little known yet accomplished Mike Ghaida [www.franchising.com/mike_ghaida] whose Lebanese father made fortune from Nigeria but who upon arrival in the United States had to hustle for success spot working his way up the franchising ladder from a pizza delivery boy and through practicing the simple principles of making the difference became very wealthy.

But the rags-to-riches success stories are not exclusive to immigrants. There are countless other inspiring stories of the likes of industrialists Andrew Carnegie and Henry Ford to one of America's prominent women of all time–Oprah Winfrey who have beaten the odds through sheer determination and made the enviable difference in various aspects of life.

The list is endless. These all made DETERMINED difference as they imbibed and extolled the traditional path of change.

It is a reality and beyond it, a possibility, that with determination and applying the principles of making the difference, anyone could dream and have the dream come true.

It must be ludicrous if not unthinkable why anyone, including those of the household of faith, should therefore think that they could be great, do exploits and make positive impact on their communities without first having a good grasp of what it takes to make that "determined" difference or the willingness to pay the price.

Would to God Christians that aspire to higher status and positions of responsibility and honor understand that they could as they observe the tried and tested principles of old! Would to God such listen to Paul's admonition to Timothy!

> "... the overseer [in the Church as in secular world] must be above reproach, the husband of one wife, temperate, self-controlled, respectable, able to teach, not given to drunkenness, not violent but gentle, not quarrelsome, not a lover of money..."–I Timothy 3:2-3 [ESV]

Then the Lord would have honored them and made them successful in whatever they undertook just as was the case with Hezekiah – II Kings 18:5-8

Yet still, Jesus counsels those desiring to build a "tower" in Luke 14:28-30:

> "Which one of you, when he wants to build a tower, does not first sit down and calculate the cost to see if he has enough to complete it? Otherwise, when he has laid the foundation and is not able to finish, all who observe it begin to ridicule him saying: 'this man began to build and is not able to finish.'" [NASB]

Not long ago, I read on a bill-board that's located at a strategic location on one of America's busy city streets that says it all. It read: LIFE'S SHORT CUTS–CUTS SHORT LIFE. It perhaps sounds somewhat too philosophical until you realize that today's popular life game could best be described "Quick-Fixes." This game is played every where and by almost everyone: politicians, athletes, business people, academia, families, etc. and it is addictive. What with the world of "Google" where virtually everything and anything could be discovered and referenced with relative ease! It used to be that we were taught lessons on staying at it and doing it right. We spent hours learning how to, till we became really good at it. Now we celebrate and reward short-cuts, quick fixes and more often than not, mediocres.

"Life's short cuts – cuts short life."

Oh that men and women will learn to do good planning and work hard. Oh that they would realize that hasty shortcuts lead to poverty–Proverbs 21:5

Worst still is the fact that our quest for legality and correctness overshadow decency and performance at the expense of expediency.

Apostle Paul must be looking far ahead at our day when he wrote to the Corinthians:

> "All things are lawful, but not all things are profitable. All things are lawful, but not all things edify."–I Corinthians 10:23 [NASB]

My main aim in writing this Book is to advocate the importance of Christian Character as needed virtues at the market place, in circle of friends and associates as well as in our very own communities: where all of the things we are taught at school, at Church, at seminars and conferences about making the difference are put to the social test. It is a collection of years of professional experience that I have embraced and upheld and now share with every aspiring leader.

They are my life's experience presented in book form. They are my way of giving back to the world, what I have learned from it, thus providing the "bridge" and passing the baton to aspiring leaders.

Beyond professionalism though, personality, integrity and quality must be seen as the necessary and much coveted excellence. In a world where "correctness" is fast replacing civility, it is necessary that personality, integrity and quality be accorded their rightful place when considering equally well educated individuals for recognition and promotion to leadership–in small, medium and large organizations. In a world where corruption, suspicion and hypocrisy seem to be so pervasive, personality, integrity and quality cannot be ignored. And in an economy with limited and competing resources, it behooves employers of labor and business leaders to be determined ever than before, to go beyond consideration of mere educational appellations, into seeking those with strong character traits.

Enduring character traits must complement paper qualification. Best qualified candidates must be those whose acknowledged lifestyle of integrity is not in doubt. That, to my mind, is the way to ensure the integrity and sustenance of enterprises.

One of America's time management experts and accomplished author Brian Tracy aptly puts it this way:

"The glue that holds all relationships together–including the relationship between the leader and the led is–**TRUST** and trust is based on **INTEGRITY**–Brian Tracy–Entrepreneur, Business Coach, leading expert on Management.

I couldn't agree more with Brian Tracy. Trust and integrity are indisputably inevitable, sustaining bond in every facet of our society: at school, at work and in our community. They are necessary in business just as they are in politics and sports. They hold things together for here, now and certainly lead us to an enduring future.

Whereas Christians form majority of the workers competing for those jobs in the United States–at 76% of total adult population *[American Religious Identification Survey, 2008;* http://b27.cc.trincoll.edu/weblogs/AmericanReligionSurvey-ARIS/reports/ARIS_Report_2008.pdf] and whereas they are as educationally qualified as any of their peers, it is an irony that fewer of those that profess and practice their Christian faith seldom get to be engaged, recognized and/or adequately rewarded, not to talk of being considered for position of responsibility and trust–because they lack the key principles of making the DETERMINED difference among their equals that their employers most often seek.

This Book is written principally to open the eyes of Christians that are aspiring to positions of influence and to afford them key spiritual insights laid out as principles of wisdom. Of course, it should also be read by non-Christians who desire the virtues that enable enduring fulfillment of life's goals.

Two Scriptures every reader/worker must seriously ponder over and take note of in reading this Book are found in Jesus' Parable of the Shrewd Manager found in Luke 16:10-12 and some of King Solomon's principles on how to succeed in life–Proverbs 24:3-4:

"Whoever can be trusted with very little can also be trusted with much, and whoever is dishonest with very little will also be dishonest with much. So if you have not been trustworthy in handling worldly wealth, who will trust you with true riches? And if you have not been trustworthy with someone else's property, who will give you property of your own?..." Luke 16:10-12 [NIV]

and...

"By wisdom a house is built, and through understanding it is established; through knowledge its rooms are filled with rare and beautiful treasures." Proverbs 24:3-4 [NIV]

I believe that each of us can make an enduring, "determined" difference when we have learned the simple truths of those key principles that enabled others succeed... laid out in this Book.

I believe that we can leave behind the pains of debilitating defeat and progress to harnessing the gains of the efforts in determined difference. Yes, WE CAN.

I reiterate though, that there could be no short-cuts or quick-fixes to enduring success!

"...all of the things we are taught at school, at Church, at seminars and conferences about making the difference are put to the social test."

It is my prayer that the KEY PRINCIPLES OF MAKING A DETERMINED DIFFERENCE presented in this book will help you discover the tried and tested characteristics of making a DETERMINED difference; so that not long from now, you also would have positioned yourself and be available, in the highly competitive environment, to make that "sought-after" difference.

Principally, it is my earnest desire to spur the restoration of morality, ethical foundations and accountability among aspiring leaders of our Churches, governments, businesses and body-politics.

Let's together explore these principles...

---

[1]Race To The Top–https://www.whitehouse.gov/issues/education/k-12/race-to-the-top

PRINCIPLE ONE

Determine... to Know What You Need, As Distinct From What You Want

Need–something you <u>have</u> to have
Want–something you <u>would like</u> to have
- Erin Huffstetler, [www.MyFrugalHome.com]

Do not be hasty in word or impulsive in thought to bring up a matter in the presence of God. For God is in heaven and you are on the earth; therefore let your words be few.–Ecclesiastes 5:2 [NASB]

*F*ew years ago, one of my children was fond of getting attracted to anything or anyone that fascinated her. She would listen to the radio and the sweet voice of the broadcasters and the music and stories and she would want to be a "radio" with sweet sounds. A while after, she would observe the stylish and respected work of the traffic corps: how the lady police officer would order massive trucks to stop and let smaller vehicles go by at the wave of her command. She was so fascinated that she really wanted to be a police officer. That fascination wore off couple of years down the road when she began to feel the love and care of her new kinder-garten "auntie" [as the children's teachers were called then]. This went on several weeks till one nice afternoon she returned home from school and her feelings found yet another expression. She ran up to me and said "Daddy, I really like Auntie L and will like to be a teacher when I grow up." Knowing that that sounded very much like another phase of her usual fancies, I nonetheless commended her and told her mommy and I would be there for her should that be her life goal. Of course today, after high school and college and the graduate school, she is anything but a radio, a police officer or a teacher. She seemed to have found her destiny and is happily pursuing it with passion and vigor.

The problem with kids is that they just do not know exactly what they want to be. Life to them is about fantasy and control. And don't we all, like kids, fail to know what we really want out of life? We see the Jones' doing one thing and we want to do the same. Then the Thomas' came along and doing another and we want to follow the trend. We're easily carried about and away by what others are doing.

One day, we see someone who is running and getting some publicity and we want to be a runner. Another day is a Hollywood star performing some stunt and there you go, we want to be and do the same. Like the children, we seem not to know why we are here on Earth or what we want from it.

Interestingly enough, I am not able to tell my own story when I was my daughter's age like as I have told hers here.

One thing though was the fact that upon joining the first organization that I worked for at age 19, my employers soon found out that I was a totally different personality when it came to dedication and focus. Whenever they needed a worker who would swing into action at their "beck and call," someone that would dedicate time and needed effort to assignments, I was the one. Once I was showed what to do, I convinced them that I could be trusted to continue undistracted and requiring little or no supervision. Even though my assignments at the time were simply routine in nature, I challenged myself to be the best at it. I became the go-to person usually in no distant time. And with just a high school diploma at the time, it appeared extra ordinary, four years after being hired, to be made the Head of a new Branch of the company, responsible only to the Regional Manager.

This book will encourage you to know the difference between what you want and what you need; between your wish and God's will for your life.

"Not having a dad that could "call friends" on my behalf,
I found out first-hand that if I must survive and succeed in life,
I had to go the extra mile, performing better,
above and beyond what anyone would call normal."

I came from a family that could be considered average economically. I lost my father who at the time was the sole bread-winner at age 12. I became dependent on my uncles and family members that were custodians of my dad's sparsely spread-out assets, for sustenance and for education. After completing primary education, my eldest brother, who was then a high school teacher, encouraged me to get prepared for the high school. I was admitted into high school and performed fairly brilliantly. Six years after, I was out of the high school and joined this international organization.

Not having a dad that could "call friends" on my behalf, I found out first-hand that if I must survive and succeed in life, I had to go the extra mile, performing better, above and beyond what anyone would call normal. I had to DETERMINE what I needed to be, what I required to be it, and also DETERMINE to pay the price–unswerved. Of course I enjoyed being relied upon. I enjoyed being the go-to person. Just the feeling that I was available to help and could really help meant much to me than the promise of remuneration or nomenclature. As I progressed through the ranks, I began to sense what might be my destiny. I found out that it was incumbent upon me to be able to extend help not only to co-workers, but also to my family, my community and by extension my generation. That was no little obligation.

I knew I had to go beyond the realm of the ordinary, to the realm of making a DETERMINED difference. I discovered that making a determined difference does not come cheap.

While at this first job, I learned experientially that whatever schooling and paper qualification a worker might have, without knowing the principles of making a *determined* difference, s/he was bound to "mark time" on the job, at best hoping to make defined progress – in keeping with inflation or not too far from it.

What an irony that many people today flounder for many years of their precious life, wanting to be who and what they do not know. It is a shame, in my thinking, to set oneself on the assembly line of life, to be moved only as others move, as it were, by the same measured force of progress. Worse still is the fact that family, friends and acquaintances continue to prod many, cheering them along the path they were not sure would take them to fulfillment not to talk of making any difference. It is my prayer that you, the reader, will discover your life's destiny soon enough if you have not already done so, in order to help you find out what you NEED to realize it.

Political scientist, diplomat and now elder statesman Henry Kissinger has been severally quoted as saying:

> "If you don't know where you are going, every road will get you nowhere."

How so true! Know what you want and the path to getting it!

BEFORE YOU START, YOU NEED TO KNOW...

MERE WORDS: HOT AIR

Humorously, there is a raging controversy as to the number of the words spoken by men and women daily. Neuroscientist

Louann Brizendine for example, puts the number of words spoken by a man at 7,000 compared to 20,000 by a woman [*Book: The Female Brain–2006*]. Mark Liberman, [Professor of Linguistics–University of Pennsylvania] on the other hand in his study [*Sex Linked Lexicon Budget posted online Aug. 6th, 2006*] supposes that men speak as many as 6,000 and women about 9,000 words each day. There are of course others that believe that men speak as much as 25,000 and women 50,000 and anything in-between these numbers. But the truth remains that mankind, [women included] speak words in thousands, so much so that what we speak turn out to be "noise" both in the ears of fellow men as well as in the ears of God–instead of voice.

And just as it is with so much vibes, we continue to desire many things and end up getting nothing. We would like to have state-of-the-art devices: hand-held, wall-mounted, desk-top, kitchen counter-top, etc. We want to have the latest model cars, most functional houses and in some instances, "hottest" status. We play the "catch-up" with the newest arrivals in the market and try to beat the Jones'. At no time in our history has the "race to the top" been so intense that it defies its original educational intent. And when we don't get what we want, we become stressed and distressed and in a sense, drop-outs.

"It is a shame, in my thinking, to set oneself on the assembly line of life, to be moved only as others move, as it were, by the same measured force of progress."

Interestingly though, and in spite of the struggles, our wants continue to belong in the right category of "wishful thinking" – of things never attained.

From the Bible Book of Genesis to Maslow's hierarchy of needs, to contemporary concepts of needs, mankind seemed confused as to what really constitutes NEED and what amounts to mere WANT.

WHAT IS A NEED?

Renowned psychologist Abraham Maslow [1908-70], in his paper titled: "A theory of human motivation" [*Psychological Review, vol. 50, 1943, 370-96*] suggested that there are five basic human needs: physiological, safety, belonging, esteem and self-actualization – in ascending order. Shortly after, he determined that the list was not exhaustive enough. He added three more: the need to know and understand; the need for aesthetic beauty and transcendence – the need to help others achieve their potential. Of course before Maslow – Darwin, Lamarck and several other prominent scientists and philosophers have defined what need is, ranging from what may be regarded as common-sensical to the bizarre – to say the least. Since Maslow, yet several others: psychologists, economists and academicians of differing persuasions have identified and proffered what this apparently "hard to pin down" subject of need is.

However, long before all of these scientists, a close study of the Creation story in the Bible reveals that the earth was in a state of chaos–without form, void and dark – Genesis 1. For six days, God determined what the earth needed, in precise sequence, to make the earth structurally and scientifically functional. You cannot beat the scientific and aesthetic order of LIGHT, HEAVEN [or skies], EARTH and VEGETATION, SUN, MOON and STARS, ANIMALS and BIRDS and finally HUMANS. Each one creation progressively meeting the need of reversing chaos, formlessness, void and darkness!

In this Book, I have taken the position that a need is that very thing [or set of things] necessary for livelihood in three dimensions – BODY, SOUL and SPIRIT.

Necessary in this context is the sense of being "essential". Livelihood is taken in terms "enabling" life and the three dimensions in which man was created and functions.

To meet a need therefore is to be in position to reverse "chaos", "formlessness", "void" and "darkness" that limits or threatens to limit, hurt or threatens to hurt, prevent or threatens to prevent the realization of those things that are necessary for human livelihood and exercising such influence – such that it results in blessing oneself as well as others. It also means the knowledge of right values [blessings] from wrong values.

God's definition of right/wrong values–in blessing is found in Psalm 1:1-6:

> "How blessed is the man who does not walk in the counsel of the wicked, nor stand in the path of sinners, nor sit in the seat of scoffers! But his delight is in the law of the LORD, and in His law he meditates day and night. He will be like a tree firmly planted by streams of water, which yields its fruit in its season and its leaf does not wither; and in whatever he does, he prospers. The wicked are not so, but they are like chaff which the wind drives away. Therefore the wicked will not stand in the judgment, nor sinners in the assembly of the righteous. For the LORD knows the way of the righteous, but the way of the wicked will perish." [NASB]

A man or woman that is meeting needs is that person that is not walking according to the evil dictates and counsels of the wicked, sinners and scoffers but rather delights in doing what is right – according to the dictates and counsels of the Most High. S/he is known and cared for by God and like a firmly planted tree by the river banks, is blessed continuously and made a blessing.

"To meet a need therefore is to be in position to reverse
"chaos", "formlessness", "void" and "darkness"
that limits or threatens to limit, hurt or threatens to hurt,
prevent or threatens to prevent the realization of those
things that are necessary for human livelihood and
exercising such influence – such that it results
in blessing oneself as well as others"

What's more, the man considered the wisest that ever lived – Solomon, summed up the counsel on meeting needs by right values in his Proverbs 1:10-19:

> "...If sinners entice you, do not consent. If they say, "Come with us, Let us lie in wait for blood, let us ambush the innocent without cause; Let us swallow them alive like Sheol, even whole, as those who go down to the pit; we will find all kinds of precious wealth, we will fill our houses with spoil; throw in your lot with us, we shall all have one purse," ...do not walk in the way with them. Keep your feet from their path, for their feet run to evil and they hasten to shed blood. Indeed, it is useless to spread the baited net in the sight of any bird; but they lie in wait for their own blood; they ambush their own lives. So are the ways of everyone who gains by violence; it takes away the life of its possessors." [NASB]

Meeting human needs does not come by conspiracy or subversive methodology.

Certainly men's wants could be met in ways that are both inexpedient and un-edifying, they however often turn out to be short-lived and infamous. Stealing to meet a need is nothing but stealing! Killing in order to make a social or political point is murder nonetheless! Sticking a note of "evil convenience" to a need met could not change the status of the evil or cleanse the supposed need met. Solomon must have experienced the situation when he wrote in Proverbs 6:16-19:

> "There are six things which the LORD hates, yes, seven which are an abomination to Him: haughty eyes, a lying tongue, and hands that shed innocent blood, a heart that devises wicked plans, feet that run rapidly to evil, a false witness who

utters lies, and one who spreads strife among brothers." [NASB]

Dare I say any more?

Some have argued that there have been situations where there does not appear to be specific rule or law broken by arguably subversive means. Or perhaps there is no Scripture that expressly prohibits taking a particular action when in desperation, with few or no option than to do the negative. In such situations, I have found wisdom in depending on the voice or promptings of the Holy Spirit. A true test is whether or not the situation gives inner peace in a "holy," "sensitive" heart and that when exposed to scrutiny – by the law of man or by the Word of God, does not make the actor feel condemned. I John 3:19-22 corroborate this succinctly:

> "…we know by this that we are of the truth, and will assure our heart before Him [God] in whatever our heart condemns us; for God is greater than our heart and knows all things. Beloved, if our heart does not condemn us, we have confidence before God; and whatever we ask we receive from Him, because we keep His commandments and do the things that are pleasing in His sight." [NASB]

ECONOMICS 101 AND GOD'S PERSPECTIVE:

Economics 101 teaches us that wealth is having abundance of valuable material possessions. Further definition in the financial world describes wealth as excess of riches as in net-worth. But that definition also has hidden nuances. A man living on credit card believes he is wealthy when he is able to buy what he wants and needs and flaunts it in the face of the poor. You probably know someone who lives flashy lifestyle but who, in reality, cannot be said to be wealthy by any stretch of imagination. S/he appears in the show-off mode from distance but at closer proximity, obviously lives the "empty drum" syndrome. The State is very possibly denied taxes or creditors unsettled. Or better still, where this so-called rich man/woman gives to the poor, such pittance has been laden with wrong intentions, mainly designed to subjugate the poor or curry favor through unfair, hidden, tactical agenda.

Wealth cannot be said to be it, when it has not positively impacted, blessed the possessor as well as others around it, including the State, the community and the neighbors – without ulterior motive. Wealth and appearance of wealth must also of necessity be distinguished as two separate existences. One is not equal to the other. Neither could ill-gotten riches and greed stand the test of true wealth.

What's more, in the eyes of God, this kind of person that makes social point does not score much. Jesus, teaching a superb lesson about wealth says in Luke 12:15: "...*A man's life does not consist of the abundance of things he possesses...*" He was referring to a supposed worldly rich man whose investments yielded so much he did not know what to do with them. He became possessive of his possession till he got to the point of saying to himself: "*Soul, you have had so much goods laid up in store for you for many years; now take your ease, eat, drink and be merry.*" [See Luke 12:16-21]. In every place that the story of this man would be told, he was constantly regarded as the "Rich Fool."

> "...*when all of life is past and the laid-up material riches are moth-eaten or of little value, only what is done for God's glory, His cause and His people: the truth we have spoken in life; the seeds we have sown in different forms; only these will remain and only for these we will be remembered.*"

King Solomon was ahead of the "Rich Fool" in Luke 12 to realize the futility of pleasure and possessions. Listen to what he had to say about the subject:

"I said to myself, "Come now, I will test you with pleasure. So enjoy yourself." And behold, it too was futility. I said of laughter, "It is madness," and of pleasure, "What does it accomplish?" I explored with my mind how to stimulate my body with wine while my mind was guiding me wisely, and how to take hold of folly, until I could see what good there is for the sons of men to do under heaven the few years of their lives. I enlarged my works: I built houses for myself, I planted vineyards for myself; I made gardens and parks for myself and I planted in them all kinds of fruit trees; I made ponds of water for myself from which to irrigate a forest of growing trees. I bought male and female slaves and I had home-born slaves. Also I possessed flocks and herds larger than all who preceded me in Jerusalem. Also, I collected for myself silver and gold and the treasure of kings and provinces. I provided for myself male and female singers and the pleasures of men — many concubines. Then I became great and increased more than all who preceded me in Jerusalem. My wisdom also stood by me. All that my eyes desired I did not refuse them. I did not withhold my heart from any pleasure, for my heart was pleased because of all my labor and this was my reward for all my labor. Thus I considered all my activities which my hands had done and the labor which I had exerted, and behold all was vanity and striving after wind and there was no profit under the sun." – Ecclesiastes 2:1-11 [NASB]

I want to make sure though, that the reader does not get the impression that I despise wealth. Rather, I am an advocate of getting wealth and of being a blessing to others. Also, beyond being wealthy materially, I believe in and counsel the importance of being spiritually and physically wealthy. The rich man in the Luke 12 story was only concerned with *"laying up treasure for himself on earth and was never rich towards God"* – v. 21. Whereas III John verse 2 desires for us to have the three-fold, all-inclusive wealth – BODY, SOUL and SPIRIT and to distribute to the poor and the needy – Romans 12:13 and Ezekiel 16:49-50:

> "Beloved, I pray that in all respects you may prosper and be in good health, just as your soul prospers." III John 2 [NASB]

> "...contributing to the needs of the saints, practicing hospitality." Romans 12:13 [NASB]

> "Behold, this was the guilt of your sister Sodom: she and her daughters had arrogance, abundant food and careless ease, but she did not help the poor and needy. Thus they were haughty and committed abominations before Me. Therefore I removed them when I saw it." Ezekiel 16:49 [NASB]

I believe, like in the words of the Church hymn writer– Horatius Bonar/Ira Sankey [1870/1891]: *"Fading away like the stars of the morning..."* that when all of life is past and the laid-up material riches are moth-eaten or of little value, only what is done for God's glory, His cause and His people: the truth we have spoken in life; the seeds we have sown in different forms; only these will remain and only for these we will be remembered. These will be the lasting impressions that will make the difference.

HASTENING TO MAKE DECISIONS...

Deciding on what you need might appear simplistic, but far from anything like it, it takes more than mere words or decision.

When we were infants, like my daughter when she was young, we liked the radio as it gives us uninterrupted stories and music. And we wanted to be like radio. Then we grew up a bit and liked the job of the policeman, the fire-fighter or the teacher – for whatever attraction they offered. We wanted to be a policeman, a fire-fighter or a teacher. And yet we grew up some more and our likes were anything from radio, policeman, fire-fighter or teacher. It just turned out that our desire kept changing with the perceived fancies surrounding us. But then, we get into college and we begin to look at life differently. In the few years following, we seemed to have made up our minds what we would be until we discover that our profession was not much in demand and back to school we went, in search for a new "marketable" profession. It could very well be an unending wrestle.

Decisions made in a rush, propelled by the spur of the moment most certainly are doomed to life of waste and regrets.

We cannot afford to make the decision of what we want or need in a haste.

Often when business decisions are to be made, managers have resorted to "need-based analysis" that looked into past successes and challenges, what has been developed and what areas could yet be explored. Then, the business will do its own "health check" to determine whether or not it has the capacity and capability before finally considering the effects of getting involved in the desired bigger picture.

Similar assessments are done by financial analysts as they draw up plans for prospective investors. Neither of these groups short-circuits the process. They took the time and the pains to study and be convinced of the direction to go before they swing the first step.

It remains a surprise why anyone desiring to make a determined difference would think less of what s/he needs and how to achieve it before taking the first step of pursuing his/her ambition.

Time and efforts spent on learning what we need are never considered wasted – if the right decision[s] is/are reached.

They would be, if either we failed to be realistic with ourselves, our capacities and capabilities or if we chose to make jumbled decision[s].

Imagine how the Prophet Habakkuk reacted to decision-making in his days:

> "I will stand upon my watch, and set me upon the tower, and will watch to see what he will say unto me, and what I shall answer when I am reproved. And the LORD answered me, and said, Write the vision, and make it plain upon tables, that he may run that readeth it. For the vision is yet for an appointed time, but at the end it shall speak, and not lie: though it tarry, wait for it; because it will surely come, it will not tarry. Behold, his soul which is lifted up is not upright in him: but the just shall live by his faith." – Habakkuk 2:1-4 [KJV]

Habakkuk seemed to be applying the business strategies: standing on his watch and on the tower – "health-check"; readiness to accept findings of analysis; formalizing the vision and making it available to others that may buy into it. Then he would wait on God [in prayers] both to receive confirmation of God's direction and for the appointed time to proceed with execution of the vision.

Best decisions are the ones whose analysis are well articulated, evaluated realistically and presented to God in prayers. These do not come from hasty or impulsive thoughts. They emanate from hours and days and sometimes weeks and months and sometimes years of review and praying and then re-reviewing – if and when needed. They are moments when PATIENCE is allowed to perfect her work – in ensuring our enduring success [James 1:4]

CAN HUMAN DESIRES FORM HIS DESTINY?

This question of man being the architect of his destiny has raged far too long in my opinion. The argument seemed unabated and cuts across academic, social and religious divide. It is an irony that many presumed intelligent people believe that they have the ability to choose their path and fulfill their destiny–all by themselves. While any one may be able to choose what s/he desires out of life, it is not left to anyone to fit that desire into his/her destiny. Rather, as we discover our destiny can we begin to fashion out what we NEED to fulfill it. In the process of writing this Book, I came across a very good book on the subject of destiny that I thought explains this succinctly. Titled "Pathways to Destiny" and written by Taiwo Ogbomo, I sincerely recommend it to whoever wants to know more about the subject of Destiny. He lays out what every man's purpose on earth is and how to fulfill that purpose. Notwithstanding, the Book of Wisdom [the Bible] gives us sufficient leads as to who we are and why we are here. Hear what God said to Jeremiah:

> "Before I formed you in the womb, I knew you. Before you were born, I set you apart for my holy purpose. I appointed you to be a prophet to the nations." Jeremiah 1:5 [GWT]

At the risk of being referred to as disparaging, I am hoping that the reader would allow me to define what the Scripture is saying here, which by the way is true of all God's creation: the word "before" means "prior to." "Knew" means being "familiar with" or "certain about something." "Before being born," to my mind, does not appear to require further interpretation. However, being set apart for a purpose is the ultimate intention here and it means what it says–"being *determined* to meet a particular need." And in the particular reference to Jeremiah, to be a prophet!

Paul the Apostle certainly was not uninformed about the matter of destiny. You could read his side of the story in Galatians 1:15-16 and Romans 1:1:

> "But even <u>before I was born,</u> <u>God chose me</u> and called me by his marvelous grace. Then it pleased him to reveal his Son to me so <u>that I</u> <u>would proclaim the Good News about Jesus</u> to the Gentiles..." [NLT]

> "Paul, a servant of Christ Jesus, <u>called to be</u> <u>an apostle</u> and <u>set apart for the gospel of</u> <u>God</u>—" [NIV]

Prophet Isaiah was another example. In chapter 49 verse 1 he says:

> "Listen to me, O islands, and pay attention, you peoples from afar. The LORD called me from the womb; from the body of my mother He named me..." [NASB]

The Bible is replete with the stories of several other people who knew that their destiny was tied to God's choice: All human-kind [Genesis 1:26-30]; Job [Job 10:8]; David [Psalm 139:14-15]; the professional smith [Isaiah 54:16]; the clay in the hands of the Potter [Jeremiah 18:1-12]; the Living creatures before God [Revelation 4:11] and many more. They knew that they were created/formed... and more so, for specific purposes!

In spite of human evaluations or need-based analysis that many mis-take for their destiny, mankind may turn to God for His will and purpose for living. A life lived outside of God's will and destiny is most often fraught with failure and stress.

O that all Christian men and women, like the royalty and peculiar beings that they rightfully are, would search out their destiny from God...

"It is the glory of God to conceal a matter, but the glory of kings is to search out a matter." Proverbs 25:2 [NASB]

Yet, somehow we all find it easier to jump into what we want instead of seeking what God needs us to be or do. We could only discern God's destiny for us: what He created us for, and working with Him to actualize it. Without any dispute, there are specific roles for each of God's creation. It is our choice by the leading of the Holy Spirit, to seek God in earnest prayer, through sound counsel from His Word and through godly people, to discover His perfect will and destiny for our lives.

To many who would rather just wake up and determine what they want to do or be, God's word to such is a resounding "Be careful..." Here is what God said to Prophet Jeremiah for example:

"And seekest thou great things for thyself? seek them not: for, behold, I will bring evil upon all flesh, saith the LORD: but thy life will I give unto thee for a prey in all places whither thou goest." - Jeremiah 45:5 [KJV]

God knew you and He is saying to you:

"But now, this is what the LORD says–He who created you, O Jacob, He who formed you, O Israel: 'Fear not, for I have redeemed you; I have summoned you by name; you are mine.'" Isaiah 43:1 [ESV]

"But you are a chosen people, a royal priesthood, a holy nation, a people belonging to God, that you may declare the praises of Him who called you out of darkness into His wonderful light." I Peter 2:9 [NIV]

*"O that all Christian men and women,
like the royalty and peculiar beings that they rightfully are,
would search out their destiny from God."*

If you will determine to wait on the Lord and let Him minister to your heart and allow Him determine the direction, as He will always do when we present ourselves without disguise, you could be rest assured that He will show you your life's destiny. Your journey through life, when directed by Divine mandate, will be focused and faster and certainly far less painful. Only then could you truly make the "determined" difference.

PRESUMPTIONS

Possibly one of the most serious prayers each of us ought to pray daily is the prayer against presumptions. What we supposed we saw but only imagined; what we thought we heard but is only our inner idea; all combined to mess up the cleanest "unsuspecting" saint.

In this day and age, when nuances; social and political correctness are presented in coloration of grey, the Christian cannot but be watchful in the matter of presumption. We cannot afford to stay off our guard. We cannot presume we know, when in actual fact we don't.

The truth be told: there are a lot of people who are pretty intellectual around us. When we make-believe that we know and in reality don't, we would have sinned presumptuously and made ourselves fall under the curse of deception.

You probably remember the story told in Mark 11:12-14, 20-21. Jesus was hungry as He approached Jerusalem. He saw the fig tree that "appeared" like it has fruits on it. But, contrary to appearance, it had nothing. Sure enough, Jesus considered it deception and cursed the tree to death!

To God, thoughts are the words that we speak; but the words can be mere hot air, if not copied from careful thoughts.

Our words must come from composed heart, not from unthought-of, hasty, prideful, immature emotions. These will of a surety lead to sin and curse.

> "He who restrains his words has knowledge, and he who has a cool spirit is a man of understanding." – Proverbs 17:27 [NASB]

We owe it to ourselves not to think only once but twice in the light of "guaranteed" consequences. David was our good example. He heard God spoke to him once but he pondered it twice – Psalm 62:11. Apostle James was another. He counseled in James 1:19 to be "quick" to hear and "slow" to speak – just so we do not fall into the sin of presumption.

Let's take God seriously and be reverent before Him. Let us put God where He rightly belongs: our Almighty God, the One who dwells in Heaven – far above all. Let's acknowledge Him and be conscious of what we say. When it comes to God and godly living, let us say what we mean and mean what we say. Let's keep our words few and purpose driven in righteousness, not in unnecessary, repetitive outbursts of "hot-air".

We all need God to guide our hearts and mouths from presumptuous sins. David and many others like him that made determined difference among their generations took the matter of presumption seriously. One of David's most powerful prayers was:

> "... keep back Your servant from presumptuous sins; Let them not rule over me; then I will be blameless, and I shall be acquitted of great transgression. Let the words of my mouth and the meditation of my heart be acceptable in Your sight, O LORD, my Rock and my Redeemer." – Psalm 19:13-14 [NASB]

- -

PRINCIPLE TWO

Determine... to Be Resolute: Firm; Not a Yo-Yo; Not yielding to negating influences or circumstances

Resolve to perform what you ought; perform without fail what you resolve.
                    Benjamin Franklin, [1706-1790].

"[The man who will receive anything from the Lord] ... when he asks, he must believe and not doubt, because he who doubts is like a wave of the sea, blown and tossed by the wind. Such a one should not think he will receive anything from the Lord; he is a double-minded man and unstable in all he does." – James 1:6-8 [NIV]

*F*ew years ago, I lived in a neighborhood overseas where there were constant commotions. It might be the fear of armed robbery on a particular day and the rumor of abductors the next. That neighborhood was so panic-stricken, people ran helter-skelter most days not even knowing what the matter was. Life in that community was unbearable to say the least. But my children never thought anything serious of it. They were constantly at peace and with all the commotion could go stay glued to television or go undisturbed to bed. On one of such days, my children saw through the window at some distance, a crowd of people running in obvious panic. I was attracted to the children's outburst of laughter. When I asked what was amusing them so much, they pointed to the crowd. I said to them that it might not be a laughing matter after all and that we needed to be on the look-out ourselves. One of them hilariously said to me "Daddy, don't worry, should for any reason there is real trouble, we must just follow the crowd. We must go with them and do whatever they are doing." I thought to myself: "what an interesting philosophy!" Follow the crowd, flow with the crowd. What the children did not know then was that the panic moves may have been orchestrated by people who would turn around in the opposite direction, to exploit those that were running. Shops were often looted in the pandemonium, houses were broken into and valuable properties stolen.

> *"…irresolute individuals are only serving the role of puns in the chessboard of the stronger-willed."*

It is pretty much the same when "floaters" are around. They are weak-minded as they constantly change minds on issues that are important to their identity. They cannot be held to a particular ground or opinion–medium-term, not to talk of long-term. In the process, they are often exploited by others more determined than they are. Even when they present themselves as being helpful, irresolute individuals are only serving the role of puns in the chessboard of the stronger-willed. They let themselves be used up and as the toothpaste tube, disposed after use. Yo-yo individuals would help others climb the ladder and let those they helped take the ladder away. Worse still, they are threatened by external influences that they see as hindrances to their achievement.

Truth be told, the fact that people never stick with a particular cause or be tenacious when duty calls or persevere in the face of adversity have been responsible for the lack of or little achievement by many. They are also the reason they cannot be depended upon. They provide the answer why they cannot qualify for positions of responsibility. They are up and down and in and out: you just can't seem to be able to hold them down.

You need to determine to be resolute. Firm. Not constantly changing. Not chameleon-like.

In today's world of constant challenges, we just must not be otherwise but resolute. It is important that we hold out and stay the course – in scarcity as in abundance; in failures as in successes.

There were times in my own life that I have had to make critical decisions. For example when I consider that I have stayed at a particular spot at workplace far too long than necessary and seemed merely to be marking time, without any hope of change in sight, I knew it was time for major decision. Some of those moments when I tried to play the "nice boy," I was disappointed since no one recognized my nicety and therefore had nothing to show for it. It was necessary that I applied the scalpel: cutting off what I thought were unhelpful saplings in form of contacts and relationships. I did not hesitate. In my case, I often fall victim of unsavory friendships. I knew that if I did not cut them off, they will eventually not only cut me off, they will cut me down. As should be expected and as highly as I held some of those friendships, I had to do the needful: cut them off. As I matured, I learned the hard way to not hesitate to break ranks with those I saw as "users." Of course I got a lot of flaks for such decisions, but in the long run, it made me more resolute. I was convinced that there could be no going back and certainly no second thoughts if I must move to my next level. For me, it was my way of responding to Jesus' saying:

> "... no man, having put his hand to the plough, and looking back, is fit for the kingdom of God."   – Luke 9:62 [KJV]

They were in my past as baggage and I was not prepared to take them into my future as excess baggage.

CHOICES… DECISIONS

We all are confronted daily with many issues of life. Whether it is with family or work or health or status or relevance or a myriad of others, we make decisions that come from our choices.

How so true that the end result of a man's life here on earth will always be the sum total of the choices and *decisions* he made! Some of those decisions we made consciously and others subconsciously. Some of the decisions are hard and sufficiently important and yet others simple and inconsequential.

As I grew up and began to understand what I consider as my destiny, I was constantly faced with flurry of options from which I had to choose the path that I felt best suited my dream. Few times, I have been mistaken in choosing from the many shades of grey and had to retrace my steps; but most often, I have been right by God's grace, and so have stuck to the decisions that I made.

> *"…to not make a choice out of the fear of failure*
> *is to deliberately make the choice to fail."*

A young beautiful lady might have several interested men that would want her hand, but only one can be the suitor. Of course you could not tell who that best suitor is from mere looks. You employ gut feeling, you ask to know a bit more about the fellow, his family and his background; and if you are a Christian, you combine all of that with PRAYERS, asking God for direction. You finally made the choice of one among many and hopefully decided a period of courtship and marriage counseling and possibly not long after, you headed for the "I do" altar. I would question your sincerity, if after you have gone through these hoops, you then turn around and decided to divorce and to pick another man from your list of interested individuals or even from elsewhere.

As absurd as my analogy might appear, that looks precisely like what many do. They look at many scenarios at work and in relationships; they stayed and slept and claimed to have prayed over choices; and in some instances even sought counsel of others they considered more experienced. They would look and perhaps wear out all options, but they just could not and have not made up their minds at the end of the day. They did not decide the direction to follow. What a waste of time and resources.

In instances where I found several look-alike "grey" choices, I have determined to pray to God and to listen to the voice of the "Holy Spirit" within and if I could benefit from counseling, have sought one, and so would make choices followed by sound decisions that I never have regretted.

I remember how when I was transitioning from the first organization that I worked for to the one I later worked for about thirty years. I had few options: There were couple of offers from companies that have heard about my dedication and thoroughness and having the openings in their organizations, were desperate to attract me on-board. One of them was a close rival of the company that I was working for. I looked at the politics of working for competition. Perhaps this company only wanted me in order to spite my current employer. The other was a large international company. On the surface, I could not imagine myself qualified to go work for an organization where I would only be a little speck among several "big wigs."

"An irresolute person may be strong physically and yet not excel. He may be intelligent but remains subservient to the dullard. He may be rich and yet be a nonentity."

I received accelerated rise to supervisory and to a good extent, independent role in the company I was working for and was well regarded. Based on the level of customer relations I had built within my short space of being promoted, I had the option of starting a new company on my own, possibly with the involvement or partnership with those friends that I had made. But then, I had the far less stressful option of staying on at the enviable position that I was and do nothing about the opportunities. I had the choice and after prayerful consideration and seeking counsel from valuable friends and discounting the ones that made me fear, I chose to go with the large organization that I was later to be exposed to greater opportunities, was promoted to the Chief Executive level some years later and was made relevant on many sides and on a much global level. I did not look back and I have never regretted that singular decision.

To me, not to make a choice at such critical time of my life out of the fear of failure was to deliberately make the choice to fail.

David, renowned King of Israel and one of the greatest prolific psalmists that ever lived wrote in Psalm 15:4 as he considered who may qualify for upward mobility among men as with before God, puts it, among several others, this way:

"… he that swears to his own hurt and does not change."

Joshua, successor to the leadership of Israel after Moses, while making the valid point about the importance of making right choices before major decisions of life challenged the people of his day, just as he challenges us to do the same today:

> "… choose you this day whom you will serve; whether the gods which your fathers served that were on the other side of the flood, or the gods of the Amorites, in whose land you dwell: but as for me and my house, we will serve the Lord." – Joshua 24:15 [KJV]

49

Both the Old and the New Testament recognize the need for sound choices leading to sound decisions. These became resolutions others saw in men and women, dead and living that made them heroes/heroines.

No one in recorded history ever truly succeeded who had not first made right and stable decisions, emanating from right and stable choices.

I dare say that when it comes to determining making the difference, it is all about Choices and Decisions.

PICTURE PERFECT–RESOLUTIONS

It must not come as a surprise that electronic merchants successfully market their products based on the higher amount of resolutions theirs have over competition. When the resolutions are fewer, the product is regarded sub-standard and inferior. And I fully understand now why they must fight for this philosophy of visibility because sharpness and clarity of image is the new trend in cutting edge technology.

They will brag for example that "what you see is what you get" and so out-sell their competitors.

Of course, we all agree that unless you manipulate your output, what you see as input on your screen will always be what you get on your printed page!

But to my mind, this matter of resolution goes far beyond digital quality and electronics. It goes into areas of prime importance in economics, in politics as in social order. Until the recent past presidential campaigns, I did not take the subject of resolutions so seriously. But the campaigns taught me so much that I had to go back into the dictionary to discover what resolution is all about.

Thesaurus, an online-based word dictionary for example, among other things, defines resolution as: solution, upshot, outcome... It also describes it as: decision, motion, promise, resolve, determination...

The internet search engine, Google describes resolution as: a firm decision to do or not to do something...

These all imply steadfastness as character and lifestyle that could in every way be likened metaphorically to a sharp and clear "picture quality".

Because I have had to deal with shades of grey life choices in many instances, sometimes in areas that others would "say" and "do" things that I know were below per and were never called to question, I have had to choose whether or not to throw my Christian ethics to the wind, join the band-wagon and receive temporary satisfaction. But one of the recent past presidential campaigns reinforced my determination to continue to be resolute and firm – without being offensive or unreasonable. I have taken the side of "others may, I will not."

If Presidential aspirant Mitt Romney had been faulted for flip-flopping by his co-party aspirant John McCain in 2007, the "accuser" would have been the saint if he had not in 2012 flip-flopped himself by endorsing Mitt at New Hampshire. And as I write, the gun control debate is fiercely raging and the National Rifle Association [NRA] is not making it easier by the flip-flopping either. First was NRA's endorsement of the need for some level of control and now, years later, that need had disappeared … Makes you wonder who is to really trust.

. But not to get away from the point, irresoluteness will haunt the most well meaning person: be s/he a worker, an employer, a politician or electorate.

Jesus would chide today's position seekers:

> "If you are untrustworthy about worldly wealth, who will trust you with the true riches of heaven?"–Luke 16:11 [NLT]

An irresolute person may be strong physically and yet not excel. He may be intelligent but remains subservient to the dullard. He may be rich and yet be a nonentity.

He is weak-minded even when he parades a façade of strong-will; he is doubt-filled even when he makes believe; he is uncertain even when he appears confident. He is almost always hesitant and never amounting to much. Irresolute individuals, like immature men, are driven about by every wind of doctrine [Ephesians 4:14] and like the sea surf are driven and tossed about by the wind [James 1:6-8].

A resolute person on the other hand is purpose-driven, tenacious, persevering, persistent and dependable.

Every Christian would remember the story of Esther, Mordecai's niece in the Book written after her name. Her captive slave-to-queen story is a classic any day and in any age and is a good example of what being resolute is. Here was a lady whose only connection to the palace was through a gate-keeper, yet by being resolute and obedient took not only the throne and the land but saved the nation of Jews of her kingdom. You probably recollect the very popular *"If I perish, I perish."* – Esther 4:16.

Job was a resolute man. We understand from the Bible that God made a boast of Job [1:8] before Satan as: *"perfect and upright* [firm, resolute, dependable]; *one that fears God and turns from evil."* God's boast of Job was not because He blessed him with wealth and protected him as Satan surmised. It was because Job was a man whose yea was yea and nay, nay. When he was tried to the point of giving up his faith and his God, he refused. His reaction was:

> "Though He slay me, yet will I trust in Him and will maintain mine integrity before Him." – Job 13:15 [AKJV]

> "For I KNOW that my Redeemer lives and that He shall stand at the latter day upon the earth: and though after my skin worms destroy this body, yet in my flesh shall I see God."–Job 19:25-26 [KJ2]

That was a picture perfect of total resolve for God's glory.

"Even though it is wisdom to worship God and be closer drawn to Him both in time of adversity as in time of plenty,

*it seems an easier remedy to want to be drawn to God
when in need than in plenty..."*

Whenever God's people resolve on the side of bringing glory to God, He shows up. He showed up in the instances that I have just stated above: the stories of Esther and Job by divine intervention in their affairs. He showed up in the case of the three Hebrew men – Shadrack, Meshach and Abednego in the seven times heated fire as the One in the likeness of the Son of God – Daniel 3:24-25. He even showed up in the case of the prodigal son when he resolved to return from his prodigious living – Luke 15:20-24.

Any time that God's people resolve to obey His call upon their lives, He shows up in a supernatural way and is honored by it. Would you? You should be rest assured that your resolution will always pay big dividends as it did with those aforementioned. Be steadfast, unmovable. The storm will not overflow you neither will fire destroy you – Isaiah 43:1-2.

Whoever that must make a determined difference cannot therefore but learn to be resolute, unwavering, abounding in his faith, ready as it were, to take on challenges even at the peril of his/her life.

Choose God and be resolute!

RISING, FALLING, RISING… HOPE

I learned the lyrics of one of the most popular Children's Sunday School songs recently. It is the song: "Father Abraham Had Many Sons…" That song has never failed to thrill children. No wonder it also thrills me. I like the idea of joining everyone, swinging and stretching, smiling and joyful to praise the Lord with my right arm, left arm, right foot, left foot, chin up, turn around and finally sitting down! It also does wonders in getting the children to stay quiet and focused afterward. Perhaps that's the more reason I like it: because after I have sang it, I seem to have done some exercise and are now ready to sit and be focused on the business of the day.

53

In my opinion though, whoever produced the song certainly deserves an award for creativity. It really fascinates me so much that I many nights hum it [sorry, am rocked by it] to bed.

But the story of Father Abraham is what the song triggers most in my mind. I consider that if I truly desire to be, as I claim, one of the many sons of Father Abraham, I owe it to myself to know who he was or at least to know some of the characteristics of this Patriarch.

His story is told in chapters 11:26-25:18 of Genesis. He had an outstanding relationship with God and trusted Him for everything. When God promised Abraham he would be blessed with seeds, like the stars of heaven, He was looking far beyond the eight biological sons [Ishmael (Genesis 16:3); Isaac (Genesis 21:5); Zimran, Jokshan, Medan, Midian, Ishbak and Shuah (Genesis 25:1-2)] that came from his loins. The Scripture recorded that Abraham: *"...believed in the Lord..."* – Genesis 15:5-6. And when after twenty-five years of waiting on the promise Abraham had Isaac, he and Sarah his wife celebrated.

But then, as the lad grew into a young adult few years later, Abraham's faith was being tried when God asked him to:

> "take your son, your only son Isaac, whom you
> love, go over to the Mount of Moriah and offer
> him there for a burnt offering..." [ESV]

Again we are told:

> "Abraham rose up... and went to the place of
> which God had told him." – Genesis 22:1-3 [KJV]

So, now I see three distinct characteristics of Father Abraham – *faith* to believe God, *patience* to endure when there seemed to be no hope and time seemed not on our side and *obedience* to doing whatever God commands, born out of loyalty to Him–among many other virtues recorded in the pages of the Bible for Abraham. These same three vital qualities would produce HOPE in Abraham's spiritual sons and daughters that would dare to exercise them – in trying times as well as in good! Paul, the Apostle was referring to Abraham's faith, patience and obedience to God when in Romans 4:18 he said:

> "Against all hope, Abraham in hope believed and
> so became the father of many nations, just as it
> had been told him: "So shall your offspring be."–
> Romans 4:18 [NIV]

Abraham's faith, patience and obedience, crystallizing in Hope, made God swear by Himself in fulfilling the promise to Abraham–Hebrews 6:13-15

Nehemiah was another. He was ridiculed by detractors, yet refused to be distracted. He was conspired against and falsely accused, but determined not to respond. He was buffeted on all sides by those he thought were friends, yet he would not bulge. He was threatened by opposition, yet he did not revenge. And when they could not get him, they tried "Temple deceit:" *"The enemy is after you to kill you"* they said. *"Let us go into the temple and hide..."* [Nehemiah 6:10].

Instead of responding in fear and acquiescing to what might be regarded as brotherly betrayal, Job's reaction was:

> "Why should I flee? And who is there, that being
> as I am, would go into the temple to save his life?
> I will not go in." – Nehemiah 6:11 [AKJV]

It was as if Nehemiah lived in the Shakespearean era when he described cowards as "dying many times before their death."

Nehemiah did not only build the broken walls of Jerusalem, he deservedly became the substantive Governor of the kingdom!

Job's story continues to be peculiar in the lessons on not yielding to negating influences or circumstances – no matter how severe. Job suffered staggering losses: Servants, unspecified number of oxen and asses [Job 1:13-15]; Servants and 7,000 sheep [Job 1:16 (v.3)]; Servants and 3,000 camels [Job 1:17 (v.3] and Servants, sons, daughters and his ranch house [Job 1:18-19]. He was never a man that would run or deny his faith at the slightest threat of trial. He refused to bend or bow because of negating influences and circumstances. Rather, he trusted God and acknowledged Him as the One that knows all about him. He had hope.

We read that in all of these losses:

> "Job arose... and worshipped; and said: 'Naked came I out of my mother's womb, and naked shall I return thither: the Lord gave, and the Lord hath taken away; blessed be the name of the Lord.' In all this Job sinned not, nor charged God foolishly." – Job 1:20-22 [KJV]

He was convinced that if God would give HOPE to a fallen, taken-for-dead tree, He could restore his losses:

> "For there is hope of a tree, if it be cut down, that it will sprout again, and that the tender branch thereof will not cease." – Job 14:7 [KJV]

True to form, God restored Job and blessed his later end than his beginning... Job 42:12-13. Only faith, patience, obedience could produce such a solid HOPE.

"Why should I flee? And who is there, that being as I am, would go into the temple to save his life? I will not go in."
– Nehemiah 6:11 [AKJV]

I could attest that many are the afflictions of the righteous. But God... will sustain the righteous who will dare to stand his ground and not give in or give up.

It is never strange to feel down, distressed and distracted when the going is not so good. Many honest successful Christian people will tell you how so many times they have been in the rot but refused to stay in the rot. One observation though has been the fact that it is the very unpleasant circumstance of life that most often draws us closer to God or some other external help. Desperation and lack have their way of making us reflect on how and why we missed it and the path to getting us back on track – if as Christians we will be perceptive and not reclusive. And even though it is wisdom to worship God and be closer drawn to Him both in time of adversity as in time of plenty, it is without question that it is an easier remedy to want to be drawn to God when in need than in plenty: when the cravings for physical pleasure and the things that we see and the pride of our achievements and possessions cloud our sense of values and beg for our attention.

Perhaps someone needs to remind us that the momentary sufferings and trials that confront us are nothing compared to the glory awaiting us – if we would through faith, patience and obedience choose to Hope.

No one has made a difference who has not first determined to stay steady in the face of threats, temptations and trials. Successful men and women have been those who by integrity have stood by what they say and do. They may stumble and fall at some point in their social or spiritual lives, but they have God's assurance they will rise! – Proverbs 24:16. They are the ones making the determined difference.

KEEP THAT STUFF... Confidence and Endurance

My mother-in-law now in the bosom of the Lord used to pay us visits from the village and would only stay few days into her promised extended rest, when she starts to miss her companions and asks to be taken back. We would laugh at her for not letting the motor engine that brought her cool off before asking to be taken back home. But something that I could never forget easily about my mother-in-law was how she would look at many of the empty bottles and cans we were disposing and would wonder why we were throwing away "those beautiful bottles [or cans]?" Should we ever say we were, she would frantically ask that we keep them for her to take back home to the village. In a matter of days, we could easily have a car trunk-load of what would have been our garbage but now, treasure to my mother-in-law. Mama always had use for stylish, colorful bottles and cans. When we would go into her house in the countryside a while later, these garbage-turned-treasures could be found standing against the walls somewhere around the house, filled with valuable items, used as simple safes and forming lines of decorative wares – by color and sizes. She found use for what we thought had completed their useful life.

> *"I was willing to be taunted, insulted and on one occasion, slapped for my new found faith."*

Looking back now, many years after her home-going, I can see why we should not be discarding some of the "signature empties" without giving thought to their extended alternative uses.

Particularly for the Christian, there have been times in our lives when we felt so strong and sometimes invincible. Perhaps we just came to know the Lord and have accepted Him as Lord and Savior. We have that awesome experience: feeling so confident nothing could go wrong now that we have the Lord in our heart and on our side. We even boast to others like Apostle Peter of old would do, that we could never go back from following the Lord, no matter what trial came our way. This pack of euphoria might last few weeks or months for some and days for others. It is possible that once the "wind of reality" begins to blow against our faith in form of trials and temptations, the euphoria soon wears off and we will begin to wonder what may have been happening to us. Yet for some, the euphoria finds its long-term meaning in an irreversible life transformation.

In my case, when I became a Christian, I was so pumped up that I thought I was much bigger and taller than my small frame. I remember how, so filled with the excitement and zeal of my new found "born again" experience I would go out during my lunch breaks to witness to my co-workers, and when I returned home in the evening, witness to family members. I was considered a nuisance and fanatic: two things I truly least was. I experienced Jesus' transformative power in my life, so much so my confidence level in Him defied any rational explanation. I was willing to be taunted, insulted and on one occasion, slapped for my new found faith. But instead of keeping back, I was the more emboldened and resolved to never trade my Jesus' experience for any other.

Today, after over forty years of been born again, I look back and can see how what others considered a nuisance that should be disposed off: my confidence, endurance and faith in Jesus Christ, have sustained me in no small measure: from those little beginnings into becoming a Chief Executive of an international company having the largest non-petroleum American investment in the entire nation, to membership of several Boards of Directors of businesses and into the enviable position of serving the Lord as a minister of the gospel. Paul was certainly right to exhort:

> "Cast not away therefore your confidence, which has great reward. For you have need of patience, that after you have done the will of God, you might receive the promise." – Hebrews 10:35-36 [KJ2]

The Christian confidence has a good payback. It enables us not to stagger or panic in the face of threats. It is the confidence and endurance that keeps us standing when challenged by the unpredictable and unavoidable vagaries of life. These motivate us to maintain our resolve never to go back to the world and its trappings. It is the same confidence, endurance and faith that set us apart to make a determined difference among many.

Keep that stuff – Confidence and endurance. You need them to make a determined difference.

Avoid distraction Be resolute and purposeful

PRINCIPLE THREE

Determine... to be strong.

Ready to perform demanding tasks and to face
challenges <u>when</u> [not if, but when] they come–
Joshua 1:9; Ecclesiastes 9:10

A child, in amazement, once asked his preacher dad:
"how come a ball bounces?" He noticed that each time
he dropped the ball, it bounces back up and interestingly too,
the harder he dropped the ball, the greater the bounce! "I drop
other things and they either break or remain on the ground.
How come that the ball is different?" the child asked his dad.
The dad thought for a moment and as if by some intuition
looked at his little lad and said to the child "that is because
of what the ball is made of. The manufacturer made the ball
specially of rubber, air-tightly blown and strong." The child
was somewhat satisfied at the dad's answer, even though he
does not seem to be able to fully comprehend what it all meant.
But the dad got a message for himself: "every Christian man
or woman who would look up to the Creator, like the ball's
manufacturer, has the ability, to resist life's hits and drops.
The harder the situation that confronts us in life, the greater
should be the ability to bounce back – if we have faith and
would trust our Manufacturer–the God of Creation and His
promises." After all, we have the assurance that we are made

specially, fearfully and wonderfully [Psalm 139:14]. We cannot and should not break. We are made STRONG. We are made in the image and likeness of God, who does not break up or bugged down by human demands–at any time.

A porcelain plate will break in pieces when dropped. A bag of sand will stay put at the very spot it is dropped. But a ball will always bounce back. And like a ball, we would not let life's trials hold us down or break us up. What's more, David the Psalmist succinctly puts it in Psalm 30:5–"weeping may endure for a night, but joy comes in the morning." We are built strong and should be strong.

A porcelain plate will break in pieces when dropped.
A bag of sand will stay put at the very spot it is dropped.
But a ball will always bounce back.
And like a ball, we would not let life's trials
hold us down or break us up.

STRONGER THAN IRON…

A while back, my one-time boss told a story about how to stay strong in the face of challenges. According to him, successful politicians are the most often good examples of strong individuals. Politicians have daunting tasks at campaign trails. They have difficult tasks in office and haunting memories after tenure. It is the successful politician that stays strong on and out of stage. Opponents cannot easily beat them down neither can criticisms break them up. They have a strong will, a will to stay up and not to be seen as weakling.

Unlike iron that can be bent under fire, a celebrated politician will not bend or be cowered under criticism – at least not when the opponent is looking for that leeway to take advantage.

A strong politician is said to have strong "codes" that cannot be easily decoded.

I soon realized though that staying strong and resilient is not characteristic of politicians alone, even though they really should be. That quality is required of everyone determining to succeed in life's many struggles.

So the question therefore is: shouldn't Christians that are aspiring to leadership position – in public as in private possess at the very least such strong qualities – if not more?

It is obvious that what makes the marked difference between many of those that succeed and those that do not has often been the fact that those who succeed stay strong and resilient in the face of challenges: criticisms and jeers and those that failed did the exact opposite: quit. The strength of those that succeeded could be seen in applause as in jeer when they remain indifferent, not being carried away by momentary elation or distress; realizing that the same crowd might, at some other point and in different situation down the road, just very well do otherwise.

The Christian worker, like every leader with sound testimonies, goes through periods of adversity and accomplishment; periods when only intimidation and threats are the necessities for strengthening him. And don't we all many times experience extreme lows and extreme highs, and are faced with decisions to stay strong and never quit? Giving in or giving up are no options. In the face of life's challenges, staying strong is.

Joshua had enemies and detractors within the camp and outside it. Israel was on its way to the Promised Land. But it was a vision transferred to him by his erstwhile leader and mentor–Moses. Admittedly it usually is easier to be strong with one's own vision and never allow distractions and discouragements to take hold. It is much tougher to keep someone else's vision on course and still be strong at it. God recognized that. How so fitting therefore it must be for the Almighty God to give Joshua this much needed psy-op ahead of the Herculean task that was ahead of him:

> "Moses my servant is dead. Therefore, the time has come for you to lead these people, the Israelites, across the Jordan River into the land I am giving them. I promise you what I promised Moses: 'Wherever you set foot, you will be on land I have given you — from the Negev wilderness in the south to the Lebanon mountains in the north, from the Euphrates River in the east to the Mediterranean Sea in the west, including all the land of the Hittites.' No one will be able to stand against you as long as you live. For I will be with you as I was with Moses. I will not fail you or abandon you. "**Be strong** and courageous, for you are the one who will lead these people to possess all the land I swore to their ancestors I would give them. **Be strong** and very courageous... This is my command — **be strong** and courageous! Do not be afraid or discouraged. For the LORD your God is with you wherever you go."–Joshua 1:2-9 [NLT]

There comes a time in all of our lives when we are faced with leadership challenges like Joshua did. Challenges differ from one person to the other. Yours might not necessarily be to lead a nation like Joshua did. Perhaps yours might be to lead few people at the workplace or at Church or within the community that you live. Whatever your challenge and however the magnitude of the call, you will always need **strength** to respond to challenges. And don't you ever think yourself totally prepared and fully adequate to face the challenges.

However, you can be rest assured that the same assurance of divine presence given to Joshua is available to you and everyone who will dare to have faith in the Almighty:

"Let your conversation be without covetousness; and be content with such things as ye have: for he hath said, **I will never leave thee, nor forsake thee.** So that we may boldly say, The Lord is my helper, and I will not fear what man shall do unto me." – Hebrews 13:5-6 [KJV]

"He is your ever present help in the time of trouble!" – Psalm 46:1 [AKJV]

PROSPERITY: FOR THE WEAK?

Don't think so. I have heard arguments from both sides of the aisle, justifying why we may not need so much strength for success – both quoting Scriptures.

The one maintains the fallibility of human strength in the face of God's omnipotence. This group stretches their reasoning, saying that God would do what He chooses, in fulfilling His plans and purposes.

The other team on the other hand embraces the need for human strength, albeit to the point of human dependency. This group, like the Greek philosopher Thales [624-526 BC] believes that only when the body is fit can the mind function as it should – notwithstanding a person's spiritual status.

Even though there are elements of truth in both stances, I am sufficiently convinced both from the history of successful individuals in the past and of course much lately, from my own life's experience, that our God can and will do anything to realize His plans and purposes. Yet He requires that we be strong, be in health and to work with our own hands.

Apostle John under inspiration prayed that Gaius might prosper, be in health even as his soul prospered [III John v.2].

King Solomon in his acclaimed wisdom noted that the race has never been to the swift nor battle to the "strong" nor bread to the wise nor yet riches to men of understanding... He nonetheless counseled to work "with all man's might [strength], because there is no other place to do that than here and when alive..." [Ecclesiastes 9:10].

65

Weakness has a companion named laziness. They relate and walk together with colleagues–complaint and complacency. It is therefore not a surprise that the Bible says in Proverbs 10:4 –

"Lazy people soon get poor; hard [*and smart*] workers get rich." [NLT]

Also Proverbs 13:4 –

"Lazy people want much but get little; but those who work hard [*and smart*] will prosper!" [NLT]

I am sufficiently convinced both from the history of successful individuals in the past and of course much lately, from my own life's experience, that our God can and will do anything to realize His plans and purposes.

CHALLENGES?

Do challenges come to all? Must we all experience challenges as part of our success story? Couldn't some "good" parent/grandparent do all the hard work, all the struggles, hustles and hassles so the offspring could just sit in and watch as the fruits of labor multiply effortlessly?

In my few experiential years, I have not heard any success story told without its share of challenges – sometimes unfair share of them. The reason many tell their success stories is because they faced challenges that were considered insurmountable by human standards and surmount they did. They paid necessary price while others were "taking it easy" expecting low hanging fruits to come effortlessly. But challenges come to us all – big and small, in our early years, as we mature and all through life.

The reality of creation from the Bible book of Genesis reveals it all. See Genesis 3:16-19:

> To the woman he said, "I will make your pains in childbearing very severe; with painful labor you will give birth to children. Your desire will be for your husband, and he will rule over you." To Adam he said, "Because you listened to your wife and ate fruit from the tree about which I commanded you, 'You must not eat from it,' "Cursed is the ground because of you; through painful toil you will eat food from it all the days of your life. It will produce thorns and thistles for you, and you will eat the plants of the field. By the sweat of your brow you will eat your food until you return to the ground, since from it you were taken; for dust you are and to dust you will return." [NIV]

I wish that mankind had a better start. Perhaps the story would be different. But that was not to be. The ground remains cursed bringing thorns and thistles and both genders toil in sweat and hardship, in pain and sorrow, before the gains came.

We all experience challenges. Some challenges last longer than others. Challenges come from our institutions, work places, communities and as if to worsen an already bad situation, challenges do not spare the sacredness of family system or the wealth of the affluent. Life just literally turned a battlefield and only those who discover and practice the enduring principles found in the spiritual laws of God seem to experience the competitive edge.

To the nature of challenges though, even though they are tests and many times threats to our advancing, they are nonetheless strengthening agents, helping to produce vibrancy and vitality when we don't give in to them.

There are few things that survive the intense heat of the desert. In spite of the sun-heated sand dunes of the desert, the intense windstorms, the lack of adequate rainfall, which make it near impossible for plant life to survive, it is my understanding that trees like the *Arabian ghaf* exceptionally thrive. Twisted, rough and mangled, the *Arabian ghaf* survives to take its place among prominent living trees. [http://www.give-aghaf.com/ghaf-story]

Challenges will come and when we don't give up on life or give in to challenges, they strengthen us and make us better people. They are necessary and should never be avoided.

And as if God Himself was giving us layered assurance, He said in Joshua 1:9 [NIV]:

> "Have I not commanded you? Be strong and courageous. Do not be afraid; do not be discouraged, for the LORD your God will be with you wherever you go."

Doing a brief study on Scriptures where words of encouragement were made to believers facing life's challenges, I found as many as 177 times.

There are those who suggest that there could very well be as many for each day of the year. Words like:

> **Do not fear; Do not fret; Do not be afraid; Do not be anxious; Do not despair; Do not be dismayed; Do not worry; Do not be discouraged; Be courageous; Be STRONG.**[1]

It sure is encouraging that God did not abandon us after the fall, but rather made enough provision for us to overcome challenges when they come! These encouragement in times of trials are sufficiently reassuring to anyone who will take advantage of them, realizing that Jesus Christ, like our other faith forerunners, went through challenges, so that we also might learn and be prepared to help ourselves and others with whom we live and those that will come after us:

> "For we have not an high priest which cannot be touched with the feeling of our infirmities [challenges]; but was in all points tempted like as *we are*, yet without sin. Let us therefore come boldly unto the throne of grace, that we may obtain mercy, and find grace to help in time of need." – Hebrews 4:15-16 [KJV]

I can attest from my own life's experience and others that I have talked with along the way, that enduring victory over challenges comes through staying strong in faith, having courage and by keeping and meditating on God's Word. Could it be that the reason we often fail to realize our call and life's ambitions is because we refuse to be strong and courageous – in our spirit, soul and body? When we allow the feeling of fear, disillusionment and low self-esteem take hold of us; when we are blown in different directions by emotions that we should never have allowed, needless to say that we lose confidence and the grip of success. Our trust in God then becomes questionable and what should fear us become what we fear, including challenges.

Challenges will come and when we don't give up on life or give in to challenges, they strengthen us and make us better people.

IT'S NOT MY BUSINESS

As I grew up, I often hear the Everybody, Somebody, Anybody and Nobody story, so much so that whenever I attended a business meeting I anticipated and could almost bet that the speaker will tell it. I'm sure you've heard the story told few times yourself. But as ludicrous as the story might sound whenever it is told, it is quite so true that majority of people today still play so true to it. When there was that important job to do, Everybody still feel convinced that Somebody would do it; and even though Anybody could have done it, it just turned out that Nobody did it. Somebody got angry about the job not being done, because it was Everybody's job. Everybody thought Anybody could do it, but Nobody realized that Everybody wouldn't do it. It ended up that Everybody blamed Somebody when Nobody did what Anybody could have done. How so funny but true today – as it has always been! "It's not my business."

The "Preacher" Solomon back in the Bible Book of Ecclesiastes 9:10 recorded what I consider a masterpiece – a thousand years before Christianity was born. Hear him:

> "Whatever your hand finds to do, do it with all your might, for in the realm of the dead, where you are going, there is neither working nor planning nor knowledge nor wisdom." [NIV]

The word "might" in the passage is the same as "ability," "power," "capacity" or "strength."

What a difference it would make if Everybody, Somebody, Anybody and Nobody do whatever they found to do or better yet, called to do! What a paradise the world would be! But it needs no arguing the fact that we all wait for someone else to do what we consider the other person could and assume should do what we could do. But the Book of Wisdom would have none of that. It says "Do It..." and "Do It With... Might [or strength]."

Because of the fear that the world would "pass the buck" does not push me to take on responsibility. I accept responsibility because I refuse to pass the buck, neither would I refuse responsibility because it was dumped on me after finding no one wanting to do it. If a responsibility was necessary to be done and I have the ability and capacity to do it, be rest assured that I will. I will make the offer at the very least and be willing and ready to do it – if it remained undone. Most times, my up-front-ness has endeared and encouraged others to join in or been emulated. What if I waited instead for Mr. Somebody to come? I am convinced that I would have played to the folk-lore and "Nobody" would have done it.

I could recount on one occasion many years back, how I had gone ahead to do what was necessary to be done because the "Somebody" to do it was not forthcoming. It was a scary job that could best be handled by an expert; but seeing that we were losing valuable dollars each passing day – waiting, I went ahead to do it to the amazement of bystanders. The company's higher hierarchy heard what I did and being impressed at my accepting such risky responsibility, noted it as exceptional bravery. The rest is now history. But suffice to say that it was the beginning of my upward movement into top management.

"Whatever your hand finds to do, do it with all your might..."

I believe with Ecclesiastes 9:10 that we can and must needs make a difference here on Earth because we would have no need for making a difference in Heaven. This is our place of opportunity to work with the talents bestowed on us – in order to show forth God's glory. What with each one's distinctiveness? Each one's ability? Each one's strength?. I am reminded of Jotham's story in Judges chapter 9. Each of the trees in his story seems to know why it is created: to offer sweetness, to cheer and honor God and man. But mankind itself? Doubtfully so.

All down the ages, God continues to seek for people that will stand in the gap, fill the void, take on responsibilities. He found Abraham as the "father" of many that will be blessed through faith. He found Moses and sent him as Israel's "deliverer" from the Egyptian oppression. Ruth was found "faithful" enough in spite of the loss of a husband and journeying to unknown people, to become the great, great grand mother of Jesus. David was a humble "shepherd" turned King. He delivered Israel from the threats and taunts of Goliath. Isaiah was not a prophet when God found him, cleansed his filthy lips and sent him to "prophecy" to his generation. Daniel. The disciples of Jesus. Paul the Apostle. The list is endless! God found these men and women and He is still looking for people to take on necessary business today.

> "… I sought for a man among them, that should make up the hedge, and stand in the gap before me for the land…" – Ezekiel 22:30 [KJV]

Will you make yourself available? Will you be ready to perform demanding tasks and to face challenges in the midst of the world's troubles and chaos? Will you present yourself as the hedge for the land so it doesn't get destroyed? Will you be willing to make that determined difference?

Make no mistake about it: there has never been a place for "It's Not My Business" people in God's kingdom and will never be.

A dear friend is often heard eulogizing the "no-pain-no-gain" slogan. To my friend, the sacrifice and determination in the face of risks/challenges are sure bankers for success.

Will you present yourself as the hedge for the land so it doesn't get destroyed? Will you be willing to make that determined difference?

READY FOR BATTLE

I like Gideon's most-unlike-it report of the 300 soldiers–National Defense team that went against the regional armies of the Midianites, Amalekites and the children of the East. 300 against so many–said to be "like grasshoppers for multitude; and their camels without number, as the sand by the sea side for multitude." You can read the account in Judges 7.

What distinguished the few soldiers and gave them the resounding victory over the multi-regional armies was the fact that they were battle-ready. There were those in Gideon's army battalion that were fearful and afraid. Those went back at Mount Gilead. There were several others as well that bowed their knees to drink from the "testing" stream. Those also returned home. These 300 soldiers kept their heads high and their eyes focused – as if to say that they were on alert. They were ready for battle. Sure enough, when faced by the myriad of enemy hosts of the Midianites, Amalekites and the children of the East, the few, like the imaginary cake of barley bread, tumbling into the enemy tent, felling and overturning it, won over the many. These few were very much determined to make the difference and they sure did.

David the King was old and in his readiness to transition called Solomon his son [I Kings 2:1-9] for an all-time important counsel. Notice his charge to Solomon in verse number 2:

"I am about to go the way of all the earth..."
"So **be strong, act like a man...**" [NIV]

I will like to believe that David's counsel for Solomon to be strong extends to all three areas of his life: physically, mentally as well as spiritually. He needed all three for the enormous tasks ahead of him. Fitting into the shoes of a king like David could be no mean feat.

I also believe that David was cautioning Solomon of the many challenges that lie ahead of him, to which he must respond as a man. Not indifferent but stable. Not faint-hearted but courageous. Not fearful but faithful.

So it was necessary to have someone the stature of Solomon who will be strong and battle-ready.

...the few, like the imaginary cake of barley bread,
tumbling into the enemy tent, felling and overturning it,
won over the many.

Another depiction of the admonition to be strong is the story of Israel under King Asa. That account is in II Chronicles 15:1-7. The prophet Azariah went to the palace and gave King Asa a spill over how for a long time, Israel had been without a true God, without law and without a teaching priest. "In those times" Prophet Azariah said to the King, "there was no peace to anyone in the country and abroad, but continuous vexation of the spirit." All of that was now ready to change and through a determined changer – Asa.

The prophet's conditionality for realizing the change was:

> "Be ye **strong**... and **let not your hands be weak:**
> for your work shall be rewarded." [KJV]

That was the same pattern for making a difference in Zechariah 8:9 –

> "thus saith the Lord of hosts: **Let your hands be strong,** ye that hear in these days the words by the mouth of the prophets..." [KJV]

That same principle is reiterated in Haggai 2:4-5 –

> "... **be strong,** O Zerubbabel, saith the LORD; and **be strong,** O Joshua, son of Josedech, the high priest; and **be strong,** all ye people of the land, saith the LORD, and work: for I am with you, saith the LORD of hosts: According to the word that I covenanted with you when ye came out of Egypt, so my spirit remaineth among you: **fear ye not.**" [KJV]

I love the assurance from God's Word for those that will stay strong, steady and determined:
"The wilderness and the solitary place shall be glad for them; and the desert shall rejoice, and blossom as the rose. It shall blossom abundantly, and rejoice even with joy and

singing: the glory of Lebanon shall be given unto it, the excellency of Carmel and Sharon, they shall see the glory of the LORD, and the excellency of our God.

> Strengthen ye the weak hands, and confirm the feeble knees. Say to them that are of a fearful heart, Be strong, fear not: behold, your God will come with vengeance, even God with a recompense; he will come and save you." – Isaiah 35:1-4 [KJV]

Show me a man that is battle-ready and will not quit in the face of challenges and I will show you a man that is poised for victory.

Apostle Paul exhorted similarly in 1 Corinthians 16:13:

> "Watch ye, stand fast in the faith, quit you like men, be strong." [KJV]

Also Ephesians 6:10-18 -

> "Finally, my brethren, be strong in the Lord, and in the power of his might. Put on the whole armour of God, that ye may be able to stand against the wiles of the devil. For we wrestle not against flesh and blood, but against principalities, against powers, against the rulers of the darkness of this world, against spiritual wickedness in high places. Wherefore take unto you the whole armour of God, that ye may be able to withstand in the evil day, and having done all, to stand. Stand therefore, having your loins girt about with truth, and having on the breastplate of righteousness; And your feet shod with the preparation of the gospel of peace; Above all, taking the shield of faith, wherewith ye shall be able to quench all the fiery darts of the wicked.

> And take the helmet of salvation, and the sword
> of the Spirit, which is the word of God: Praying
> always with all prayer and supplication, and
> watching thereunto with all perseverance and
> supplication for all saints." [KJV]

Simply read, it says... Be watchful; be faith-stable; be strong; be battle-ready.

Together with the qualities of vision and discipline, being strong and battle-ready are formidable ingredients of enduring success. It is my prayer that the Lord will strengthen your hands, your mind and your heart; that He will strengthen your feet and your total being – body, soul and spirit; so that when the times of tests and trials come [not if they come, but when they come] you will be battle-ready not in your power, but in dependence on the Lord, yet determined, to overcome. I pray that your hands be strengthened, so that whatsoever you shall find to do, you might do it with all your might to make the difference.

BURDEN, PASSION, FULFILLMENT

The Bible story of Nehemiah who rose from a steward to becoming one of Israel's inspiring leaders must of necessity offer powerful lesson on the need for staying strong to any and every aspiring leader.

Once told the state of his people and the nation of Israel – after captivity, how the nation and its people were distressed [Nehemiah 1:2-3], he became restless. He developed **burden** for what needs be done [v.4], then the **passion** to get it done [vv. 4-11; 2:1-8] and moved forward to getting it done, albeit strategically **[i.e. fulfillment]** [2:9 – 6:19].

This process seems a common denominator among all that have made some impact in life's many challenges: burden, passion and fulfillment, until you evaluate the degree of strength brought into the mix, and discover the extent, effectiveness and duration of success.

A widespread, accepted and enduring change would have resulted from the strength – both of character and faith of the person[s] initiating it. The reverse has always been the case when people have doubts as to the integrity of the initiator.

The strength of character and faith of Nehemiah started from the palace.

Nehemiah mattered in character and faith. He could be noticed and listened to by no less a person than the King and Queen of Persia. In wisdom he asked them both if they "… would be pleased to send me…"–Nehemiah 2:5. That was after he had prayed to the God of heaven [- 2:4].

Nehemiah certainly was not one that could be ignored. His strength of character and his faith spoke for him – at the palace before the King and Queen; among those that he had letters written to on his behalf along the way to Judah and even upon his arrival at Jerusalem among his people. His strength of character and faith spoke!

It spoke compassion, encouragement and support from sources that knew nothing about Nehemiah but that would rather see Nehemiah's vision [burden, passion and fulfillment] realized then and thereafter.

It was the strength of character and of faith that saw Nehemiah through the oppositions and struggles. It was the strength of character and of faith that made him and his team remain in constant battle readiness against the whims and caprices of their enemies and detractors.

- -

Reference:
Note[1]
- Genesis 15:1 – *After this, the word of the Lord came to Abram in a vision: '**Do not be afraid**, Abram. I am your shield, your very great reward.'*
- Genesis 21:17 – *God heard the boy crying, and the angel of God called to Hagar from heaven and said to her 'What is the matter, Hagar? **Do not be afraid**; God has heard the boy crying as he lies there.'*

- Genesis 26:24 – *That night the Lord appeared to him and said, 'I am the God of your father Abraham. **Do not be afraid**, for I am with you; I will bless you and will increase the number of your descendants for the sake of my servant Abraham.'*
- Genesis 35:17 – *And as she was having great difficulty in childbirth, the midwife said to her '**Don't despair**, for you have another son'*
- Genesis 43:23 – *'It's all right', he said. '**Don't be afraid**. Your God, the God of your father, has given you treasure in your sacks; I received your silver.' Then he brought Simeon out to them.*
- Genesis 46:3 – *'I am God, the God of your father,' he said. '**Do not be afraid** to go down to Egypt, for I will make you into a great nation there.'*
- Genesis 50:19 – *But Joseph said to them, '**Don't be afraid**. Am I in the place of God?'*
- Genesis 50:21 – *'So then, **don't be afraid**. I will provide for you and your children.' And he reassured them and spoke kindly to them.*
- Exodus 14:13 – *Moses answered the people, '**Do not be afraid**. Stand firm and you will see the deliverance the Lord will bring you today. The Egyptians you see today you will never see again.'*
- Exodus 20:20 – *Moses said to the people '**Do not be afraid**. God has come to test you, so that the fear of God will be with you to keep you from sinning.'*
- Leviticus 26:6 – *I will grant peace in the land, and you will lie down and **no one will make you afraid**. I will remove wild beasts from the land and the sword will not pass through your country.*
- Number 14:9 – *Only do not rebel against the Lord. And **do not be afraid** of the people of the land, because we will devour them. Their protection is gone, but the Lord is with us. **Do not be afraid of them**.*
- Numbers 21:34 – *The Lord said to Moses, '**Do not be afraid** of him, for I have delivered him into your hands, along with*

78

his whole army and his land. Do to him what you did to Sihon King of the Amorites, who reigned in Heshbon.'

- Deuteronomy 1:17 – *Do not show partiality in judging; hear both small and great alike.* **Do not be afraid** *of anyone, for judgment belongs to God.*
- Deuteronomy 1:21 – *See, the Lord your God has given you the land. Go up and take possession of it as the Lord, the God of your ancestors, told you.* **Do not be afraid; do not be discouraged.**
- Deuteronomy 1:29 – *Then I said to you, 'Do not be terrified;* **do not be afraid** *of them.'*
- Deuteronomy 3:2 – *The Lord said to me* **'Do not be afraid** *of him, for I have delivered him into your hands, along with his whole army and his land. Do to him what you did to Sihon king of the Amorites, who reigned in Heshbon*
- Deuteronomy 3:22 – **Do not be afraid** *of them; the Lord you God himself will fight for you.*
- Deuteronomy 7:18 – *But* **do not be afraid** *of them; remember well what the Lord your God did to Pharaoh and to all Egypt.*
- Deuteronomy 20:1 – *When you go to war against your enemies and see horses and chariots and an army greater than yours,* **do not be afraid** *of them, because the Lord your God, who brought you up out of Egypt, will be with you.*
- Deuteronomy 20:3 – *He shall say: 'Hear, Israel: today you are going into battle against your enemies.* **Do not be faint-hearted or afraid;** *do not panic or be terrified by them.'*
- Deuteronomy 31:6 – **'Be strong and courageous. Do not be afraid** *or terrified because of them, for the Lord your God goes with you; he will never leave you nor forsake you.'*
- Deuteronomy 31:8 – *'The Lord himself goes before you and will be with you; he will never leave you nor forsake you.* **Do not be afraid; do not be discouraged.'**
- Joshua 1:9 – *'Have I not commanded you?* **Be strong and courageous. Do not be afraid; do not be discouraged,** *for the Lord your God will be with you wherever you go.'*

- Joshua 8:1 – *Then the Lord said to Joshua, '**Do not be afraid; do not be discouraged**. Take the whole army with you, and go up and attack Ai. For I have delivered into your hands the king of Ai, his people, his city and his land.'*
- Joshua 10:8 – *The Lord said to Joshua, '**Do not be afraid** of them; I have given them into your hand. Not one of them will be able to withstand you.'*
- Joshua 10:25 – *Joshua said to them, '**Do not be afraid; do not be discouraged. Be strong** and **courageous**. This is what the Lord will do to all the enemies you are going to fight.'*
- Joshua 11:6 – *The Lord said to Joshua, '**Do not be afraid** of them, because by this time tomorrow I will hand all of them, slain, over to Israel. You are to hamstring their horses and burn their chariots'*
- Judges 4:18 – *Jael went out to meet Sisera and said to him, 'Come, my lord, come right in. **Don't be afraid**.' So he entered her tent and she covered him with a blanket.*
- Judges 6:23 – *But the Lord said to him, 'Peace! **Do not be afraid**. You are not going to die.'*
- I Samuel 4:20 – *As she was dying the women attending her said, '**Don't despair**; you have given birth to a son.' But she did not respond or pay any attention.'*
- I Samuel 12:20 – *'**Do no be afraid**,' Samuel replied. 'You have done all this evil; yet do not turn away from the Lord, but serve the Lord with all your heart.'*
- I Samuel 22:23 – *Stay with me; **don't be afraid**. The man who wants to kill you is trying to kill me too. You will be safe with me.'*
- I Samuel 23:17 – *'**Don't be afraid**,' he said. 'My father Saul will not lay a hand on you. You shall be king over Israel, and I will be second to you. Even my father Saul knows this.'*
- I Samuel 28:13 – *The king said to her, '**Don't be afraid**. What do you see?'*
- II Samuel 9:7 – *'**Don't be afraid**,' David said to him, 'for I will surely show you kindness for the sake of your father Jonathan. I will restore to you all the land that belonged to your grandfather Saul, and you will always eat at my table.'*

- I Kings 17:13 – *Elijah said to her, '**Don't be afraid**. Go home and do as you have said. But first make a small loaf of bread for me from what you have and bring it to me, and make something for yourself and your son.'*
- II Kings 1:15 – *The angel of the Lord said to Elijah, 'Go down with him; **do not be afraid** of him.' So Elijah got up and went down with him to the king.*
- II Kings 6:16 – '**Don't be afraid**,' *the prophet answered. 'Those who are with us are more than those who are with them.'*
- II Kings 19:6 – *Isaiah said to them, 'Tell your master, "This is what the Lord says: **do not be afraid** of what you have heard – those words with which the underlings of the king of Assyria have blasphemed me."'*
- II Kings 25:24 – *Gedaliah took an oath to reassure them and their men. '**Do not be afraid** of the Babylonian officials, he said. 'Settle down in the land and serve the king of Babylon, and it will go will with you.'*
- I Chronicles 22:13 – *Then you will have success if you are careful to observe the decrees and laws that the Lord gave to Moses for Israel. **Be strong** and **courageous. Do not be afraid** or **discouraged**.*
- I chronicles 28:20 – *David also said to Solomon his son, '**Be strong** and **courageous**, and do the work. **Do not be afraid** or **discouraged**, for the Lord God, my God, is with you. He will not fail you or forsake you until all the work for the temple of the Lord is finished.'*
- II Chronicles 20:15 – *He said: 'Listen, King Jehoshaphat and all who live in Judah and Jerusalem! This is what the Lord says to you: "**Do not be afraid** or **discouraged** because of this vast army. For the battle is not yours, but God's"'*
- II Chronicles 20:17 – *"You will not have to fight this battle. Take up your positions; stand firm and see the deliverance the Lord will give you, Judah and Jerusalem. **Do not be afraid**; **do not be discouraged**. God out to face them tomorrow, and the Lord will be with you."*
- II Chronicles 32:7 – '**Be strong** and **courageous. Do not be afraid** or **discouraged** because of the king of Assyria and

the vast army with him, for there is a greater power with us than with him.'

- Nehemiah 4:14 – *After I looked things over, I stood up and said to the nobles, the officials and the rest of the people, 'Don't be afraid of them. Remember the Lord, who is great and awesome, and fight for your families, your sons and your daughters, your wives and your homes.'*

- Job 5:21 – *You will be protected from the last of the tongue, and **need not fear** when destruction comes.*

- Job 11:15 – *then, free of fault, you will lift up your face; you will **stand firm and without fear.***

- Job 21:9 – *Their homes are **safe and free from fear**; the rod of God is not on them.*

- Psalm 3:6 – *I **will not fear** though tens of thousands assail me on every side.*

- Psalm 4:8 – *In peace I will lie down and sleep, for you alone, Lord, make me dwell in safety.*

- Psalm 16:7-9 *I will praise the Lord who counsels me; even at night my heart instructs me. I keep my eyes always on the Lord. With him at my right hand, **I shall not be shaken.** Therefore my heart is glad and my tongue rejoices; my body also will rest secure.*

- Psalm 23:4 *Even though I walk through the darkest valley, **I will fear no evil**, for you are with me; your rod and your staff they comfort me.*

- Psalm 27:1 *The Lord is my light and my salvation – **whom shall I fear?** The Lord is the stronghold of my life – **of whom shall I be afraid?***

- Psalm 27:3 Though an army besiege me, **my heart will not fear;** though war break out against me, even then I will be confident.

- Psalm 29:11 *The Lord gives strength to his people; **the Lord blesses his people with peace.***

- Psalm 37:1 *Do not fret* because of those who are evil or be envious of those who do wrong;

- Psalm 37:7 *Be still before the* LORD *and wait patiently for him;* **do not fret** *when people succeed in their ways, when they carry out their wicked schemes.*
- Psalm 37:8 *Refrain from anger and turn from wrath;* **do not fret**–*it leads only to evil.*
- Psalm 46:2 – *Therefore* **we will not fear**, *though the earth give way and the mountains fall into the heart of the sea.*
- Psalm 49:16 – **Do not be overawed** *when others grow rich, when the splendour of their houses increases;*
- Psalm 56: 3-4 – *When I am afraid, I put my trust in you. In God, whose word I praise –* **in God I trust** *and* **am not afraid**. *What can mere mortals do to me?*
- Psalm 56:11 – **In God I trust and not afraid**. *What can man do to me?*
- Psalm 78:53 – *He guided them safely, so* **they were unafraid**; *but the sea engulfed their enemies.*
- Psalm 91:5 – **You will not fear** *the terror of night, nor the arrow that flies by day,*
- Psalm 94:19 – *When anxiety was great within me,* **your consolation brought me joy.**
- Psalm 118:6 – *The Lord is with me;* **I will not be afraid.** *What can mere mortals do to me?*
- Psalm 119:165 – **Great peace** *have those who love your law, and nothing can make them stumble.*
- Proverbs 3:24 – *When you lie down,* **you will not be afraid**; *when you lie down, your sleep will be sweet.*
- Proverbs 3:25 – **Have no fear** *of sudden disaster or of the ruin that overtakes the wicked*
- Proverbs 24:19 **Do not fret** *because of evildoers or be envious of the wicked*
- Ecclesiastes 11:10 – *So then,* **banish anxiety from your heart** *and cast off the troubles of your body, for youth and vigour are meaningless.*
- Isaiah 7:4 – *Say to him "Be careful, keep calm and* **don't be afraid**. *Do not lose heart because of these two smouldering stubs of firewood – because of the fierce anger or Rezin and Aram and of the son of Remaliah."*

- Isaiah 8:12 *'Do not call conspiracy everything this people calls a conspiracy; **do not fear** what they fear, and do not dread it.'*
- Isaiah 10:24 – *Therefore this is what the Lord, the Lord Almighty, says: 'My people who live in Zion, **do not be afraid** of the Assyrians, who beat you with a rod and lift up a club against you, as Egypt did.'*
- Isaiah 12:2 – *Surely God is my salvation; I will trust and **not be afraid**. The Lord, the Lord himself, is my strength and my defense; he has become my salvation.'*
- Isaiah 17:2 – *The cities of Aroer will be deserted and left to flocks, which will lie down, with **no one to make them afraid.***
- Isaiah 26:3 – *You will **keep in perfect peace** those whose minds are steadfast, because they trust in you.*
- Isaiah 35:4 – *say to those with fearful hearts, '**Be strong, do not fear**; your God will come, he will come with vengeance; with divine retribution he will come to save you.'*
- Isaiah 37:6 – *Isaiah said to them, 'Tell your master, "This is what the Lord says: **do not be afraid** of what you have heard – those words with which the underlings of the king of Assyria have blasphemed me.'*
- Isaiah 40:9 – *You who bring good news to Zion, go up on a high mountain. You who bring good news to Jerusalem, lift up your voice with a shout, lift it up, **do not be afraid**; say to the towns of Judah, 'Here is your God!'*
- Isaiah 41:10 – **So do not fear**, *for I am with you; **do not be dismayed**, for I am your God. I will strengthen you and help you; I will uphold you with my righteous right hand.*
- Isaiah 41:13 – *For I am the Lord you God who takes hold of your right hand and says to you, '**Do not fear**; I will help you.'*
- Isaiah 41:14 – *'**Do not be afraid**, you worm Jacob, little Israel, **do not fear**, for I myself will help you' declares the Lord, your Redeemer, the Holy One of Israel.*
- Isaiah 43:1 – *But now, this is what the Lord says – he who created you, Jacob, he who formed you, Israel: '**Do not fear**,*

84

for I have redeemed you; I have summoned you by name; you are mine.'

- Isaiah 43:5 – **Do not be afraid,** *for I am with you; I will bring your children from the east and gather you from the west.*
- Isaiah 44:2 – *This is what the Lord says – he who made you, who formed you in the womb, and who will help you:* **do not be afraid,** *Jacob, my servant, Jeshurun, whom I have chosen.*
- Isaiah 44:8 – *Do not tremble,* **do not be afraid.** *Did I not proclaim this and foretell it long ago? You are my witnesses. Is there any God besides me? No, there is no other Rock; I know not one.'*
- Isaiah 51:7 – *'Hear me, you who know what is right, you people who have taken my instruction to heart:* **do not fear** *the reproach of mere mortals or be terrified by their insults'*
- Isaiah 54:4 – *'***Do not be afraid;*** you will not be put to shame. Do not fear disgrace; you will not be humiliated. You will forget the shame of your youth and remember no more the reproach of your widowhood.'*
- Isaiah 54:14 – *In righteousness you will be established: tyranny will be far from you;* **you will have nothing to fear.** *Terror will be far removed; it will not come near you.*
- Jeremiah 1:8 – *'***Do not be afraid** *of them, for I am with you and will rescue you,'* *declares the Lord*
- Jeremiah 10:5 – *Like a scarecrow in a cucumber field, their idols cannot speak; they must be carried because they cannot walk.* **Do not fear them;** *they can do you no harm nor can they do any good.'*
- Jeremiah 17:8 – *They will be like a tree planted by the water that sends out its roots by the stream.* **It does not fear** *when heat comes; its leaves are always green. It has no worries in a year of drought and never fails to bear fruit.'*
- Jeremiah 30:10 – *"So* **do not be afraid,** *Jacob, my servant;* **do not be dismayed,** *Israel," declares the Lord. "I will surely save you out of a distant place, your descendants from the land of their exile. Jacob will again have peace and security, and no one will make him afraid."*

- Jeremiah 40:9 – *Gedaliah son of Ahikam, the son of Shaphan, took an oath to reassure them and their men.* '**Do not be afraid** *to serve the Babylonians,' he said. 'Settle down in the land and serve the king of Babylon, and it will go well with you.'*
- Jeremiah 42:11 – **Do not be afraid** *of the king of Babylon, whom you now fear. Do not be afraid of him, declares the Lord, for I am with you and will save you and deliver you from his hands.*
- Jeremiah 46:27 – *'***Do not be afraid***, Jacob my servant;* **do not be dismayed***, Israel. I will surely save you out of a distant place, your descendants from the land of their exile. Jacob will again have peace and security, and no one will make him afraid.'*
- Jeremiah 46:28 – **Do not be afraid***, Jacob my servant, for I am with you; declares the Lord. 'Though I completely destroy all the nations among which I scatter you, I will not completely destroy you. I will discipline you but only in due measure; I will not let you go entirely unpunished.'*
- Jeremiah 51:46 – **Do not lose heart or be afraid** *when rumours are heard in the land; one rumour comes this year, another the next, rumours of violence in the land and of ruler against ruler.*
- Lamentations 3:57 – *You came near when I called you and you said.* '**Do not fear**.'
- Ezekiel 3:9 – *I will make your forehead like the hardest stone, harder than flint.* **Do not be afraid** *of them or terrified by them, though they are a rebellious people.*
- Daniel 10:12 – *Then he continued,* '**Do not be afraid***, Daniel. Since the first day that you set your mind to gain understanding and to humble yourself before your God, your words were heard, and I have come in response to them.'*
- Daniel 10:19 – *'***Do not be afraid***, you who are highly esteemed,' he said. 'Peace!* **Be strong** *now;* **be strong***;' When he spoke to me, I was strengthened and said, 'Speak , my lord, since you have given me strength.'*

- Joel 2:21-22 – **Do not be afraid,** *land of Judah; be glad and rejoice. Surely the Lord has done great things!* **Do not be afraid,** *you wild animals, for the pastures in the wilderness are becoming green. The trees are bearing their fruit; the fig-tree and the vine yield their riches.*

- Zephaniah 3:16 – *On that day they will say to Jerusalem,* **'Do not fear,** *Zion; do not let your hands hang limp.'*

- Haggai 2:5 – *"This is what I covenanted with you when you came out of Egypt. And my Spirit remains among you.* **Do not fear."**

- Zechariah 8:13 – *'Just as you, Judah and Israel, have been a curse among the nations, so I will save you and you will be a blessing.* **Do not be afraid,** *but let your hands* **be strong.'**

- Zechariah 8:15 – *'so now I have determined to do good again to Jerusalem and Judah.* **Do not be afraid.'**

- Matthew 1:20 – *But after he had considered this, an angel of the Lord appeared to him in a dream and said 'Joseph son of David,* **do not be afraid** *to take Mary home as your wife, because what is conceived in her is from the Holy Spirit.'*

- Matthew 6:25-34 – *Therefore I tell you,* **do not worry** *about your life, what you will eat or drink; or about your body, what you will wear. Is not life more than food, and the body more than clothes: Look at the birds of the air; they do not sow or reap or store away in barns, and yet your heavenly Father feeds them. Are you not much more valuable than they? Can any one of you by worrying add a single hour to your life? And* **why do you worry** *about clothes? See how the flowers of the field grown. They do not labour or spin. Yet I tell you that not even Solomon in all his splendour was dressed like one of these. If that is how God clothes the grass of the field, which is here today and tomorrow is thrown into the fire, will he not much more clothe you – you of little faith? So* **do not worry,** *saying "What shall we eat?" or "What shall we drink?" or "What shall we wear?" For the pagans run after all these things, and your heavenly Father knows that you need them. But seek first his kingdom and his righteousness , and all these things will be given to you as well. Therefore do* *not worry about tomorrow, for tomorrow will worry about itself. Each day has enough trouble of its own.*

- Matthew 10:19 – *But when they arrest you, **do not worry** about what to say or how to say it. At that time you will be given what to say.*
- Matthew 10:26 – *'So **do not be afraid** of them, for there is nothing concealed that will not be disclosed, or hidden that will not be made known.'*
- Matthew 10:28 – ***Do not be afraid** of those who kill the body but cannot kill the soul. Rather be afraid of the One who can destroy both soul and body in hell.*
- Matthew 10:31 – *So **don't be afraid**; you are worth more than many sparrows.*
- Matthew 14:27 – *But Jesus immediately said to them: 'Take courage! It is I. **Don't be afraid.**'*
- Matthew 17:7 – *But Jesus came and touched them. 'Get up,' he said. '**Don't be afraid.**'*
- Matthew 28:5 – *The angel said to the women, '**Do not be afraid**, for I know that you are looking for Jesus, who was crucified.'*
- Matthew 28:10 – *Then Jesus said to them, '**Do not be afraid**. Go and tell my brothers to to go Galilee; there they will see me.'*
- Mark 5:36 – *Overhearing what they said, Jesus told him, '**Don't be afraid**; just believe.'*
- Mark 6:50 – *because they all saw him and were terrified. Immediately he spoke to them and said, 'Take courage! It is I. **Don't be afraid.**'*
- Mark 13:11 – *Whenever you are arrested and brought to trail, **do not worry** beforehand about what to say. Just say whatever is given you at the time, for it is not you speaking, but the Holy Spirit.*
- Luke 1:13 – *But the angel said to him: '**Do not be afraid**, Zechariah; your prayer has been heard. Your wife Elizabeth will bear you a son, and you are to call him John.'*
- Luke 1:30 – *But the angel said to her, '**Do not be afraid**, Mary, you have found favour with God.'*

- Luke 2:10 – *But the angel said to them, '**Do not be afraid**. I bring you good news that will cause great joy for all the people.'*
- Luke 5:10 – *and so were James and John, the sons of Zebedee, Simon's partners. Then Jesus said to Simon, '**Don't be afraid**; from now on you will fish for people.'*
- Luke 8:50 – *Hearing this, Jesus said to Jairus, '**Don't be afraid**; just believe, and she will be healed.'*
- Luke 12:4 – *'I tell you, my friends, **do not be afraid** of those who kill the body and after that can do no more.'*
- Luke 12:7 – *Indeed, the very hairs of your head are all numbered. **Don't be afraid**; you are worth more than many sparrows.*
- Luke 12:11 – *When you are brought before synagogues, rulers and authorities, **do not worry** about how you will defend yourselves or what you will say,*
- Luke 12:32 – *'**Do not be afraid**, little flock, for your Father has been pleased to give you the kingdom.'*
- John 6:20 – *But he said to them, 'It is I; **don't be afraid**.'*
- John 12:15 – *'**Do not be afraid**, Daughter Zion; see, your king is coming, seated on a donkey's colt'*
- John 14:27 – *Peace I leave with you; my peace I give you. I do not give to you as the world gives. Do not let your hearts be troubled and **do not be afraid**.*
- John 16:33 – *'I have told you these things, so that **in me you may have peace**. In this world you will have trouble. But take heart! I have overcome the world.'*
- Acts 18:9 – *One night the Lord spoke to Paul in a vision: '**Do not be afraid**; keep on speaking, do not be silent.'*
- Acts 20:10 – *Paul went down, threw himself on the young man and put his arms round him. '**Don't be alarmed**,' he said, 'He's alive!'*
- Acts 27:24 – *and said, "**Do not be afraid**, Paul. You must stand trial before Caesar; and God has graciously given you the lives of all who sail with you."*

- Romans 5:1 – *Therefore, since we have been justified through faith, **we have peace with God** through our Lord Jesus Christ,*
- Hebrews 13:6 – *So we say with confidence, 'The Lord is my helper; **I will not be afraid**. What can mere mortals do to me?'*
- Philippians 4:6 – ***Do not be anxious about anything** but in every situation, by prayer and petition, with thanksgiving, present your requests to God.*
- I Peter 3:6 – *like Sarah, who obeyed Abraham and called him her lord. You are her daughters if you do what is right and **do not give way to fear.***
- I Peter 3:14 – *But even if you should suffer for what is right, you are blessed. '**Do not fear** their threats; do not be frightened.'*
- 1 Peter 5:7 – ***Cast all your anxiety on him** because he cares for you.*
- 1 John 4:18 – ***There is no fear in love.** But perfect love drives out fear, because fear has to do with punishment. The one who fears is not made perfect in love.*
- Revelation 1:17 – *When I saw him, I fell at his feet as though dead. Then he placed his right hand on me and said: '**Do not be afraid**. I am the First and the Last.'*
- Revelation 2:10 – ***Do not be afraid** of what you are about to suffer. I tell you, the devil will put some of you in prison to test you, and you will suffer persecution for ten days. Be faithful, even to the point of death, and I will give you life as your victor's crown.*

PRINCIPLE FOUR

Determine... to Be Bold.

Ready to take Risks, Brave, Courageous –
Ephesians 3:11-12

"Whatever course you decide upon, there is always someone to tell you that you are wrong. There are always difficulties arising which tempt you to believe that your critics are right. To map out a course of action and follow it to an end requires courage." – **Ralph Waldo Emerson**

BOLDNESS

*H*ere is one of the triplet descendants of success– Boldness. The other two being Bravery and Courage. Boldness will not hesitate or be afraid when faced with possible danger, even when it meant breaking the tradition. And like one of his other sibling – courage, boldness safely dares.

Boldness in business as in leadership is a major key to success. It is a prominent virtue equated only to determination. Again, like courage, you need it to venture into opportunities and challenges.

Spiritual Boldness on the other hand makes the Christian who has an otherwise shy natural disposition confident and courageous. See Proverbs 28:1; Acts 4:13; Acts 13:46; I Thessalonians 2:2;

Spiritual boldness is developed through intimacy in relationship with God the Father, the Savior Lord Jesus Christ and the quickening Holy Spirit – Luke 11:8

Boldness is the opposite of shyness, cowardice, fear and timidity. While these produce inactivity and boredom, boldness encourages activity.

Bold people stand out from the average others around them. They are confident, courageous, and obviously directed. They instigate growth, progress, and movement for themselves and others. Yet someone suggests that boldness is the manifestation of meekness–under control.

And even though I have not quite gotten to the level of being a physical fitness enthusiast, I nonetheless embrace the philosophy of one of Florida based creators of physical fitness sportswear[1] LBD Apparel–Pedro Pertile and Camaren Walker. Their slogan somewhat inspires and aptly captures the essence of what boldness really is. According to them, you "either **live bold or die** bored." And their very one reason? TO STAND OUT from the average: i.e. make the determined difference! I kind of like that.

Boldness in business as in leadership is a major key to success.
It is a prominent virtue equated only to determination.

There is a difference between boldness and carelessness though. Bold leaders have strong self-awareness as well as surrounding-awareness. They know when and where they should take bold action, and they also know when and where they should not.

Dare I say though that worldly boldness or rather boldness not backed with spiritual sensibilities might very well be danger-laden and many times fatal?

Lions are never known to be rash even though naturally bold. They have the nerve and sensibilities enough to assess situations that are beyond their capabilities and to run off. They know their surroundings well enough to determine fight or flight. They do due diligence and measure the level of risk-to-reward and are often ready to commit based on the anticipation for positive outcome.

Could any worker aspiring to be leader do less? I don't think or believe so.

Boldness without the inner assurance, conviction and direction might very well be a show of impudence and recklessness, most often resulting in hurt.

DAVID THE GIANT

That was the character of boldness – David and Philistine's Goliath. The account in I Samuel chapter 17 actually tells of the story of two types of boldness: one by a natural giant Goliath that was intimidating, impudent, reckless and boastful; the other by a youth–David, far less the height and weight of the intimidating mountainous opponent that's fitted with frightening armor. Again, the lesson in this story could not be about the bravado of Goliath but in David's brave, fearless and courageous confrontation of the man whose scare tactics was to give way to the true champion – David. That was the man David–ready to face and actually faced the challenges head-on in spite of the apparent intimidation. Goliath may be big in body-mass but it was David that became the "real giant!" That's the character of true boldness.

You also would have read the defying story of the three Hebrew guys in Daniel chapter 3. They were bold before a conquering King known to the world then as no-nonsense-Nebuchadnezzar. Even the mere mention of his name drove fears down the spine of the most nationalistic Babylonian. That was the tradition of the time: everyone was to bow to the image at the sound of the Babylonian national anthem. The Hebrew men were threatened fiery furnace if they failed to pay obeisance to the King and his Duran statue. But because of their faith in the true God, the Creator of the Universe, that was exactly what they did – they refused to bow and they did not burn. They were confident that their God, greater and more powerful than Nebuchadnezzar would deliver them. He did. The tyrant King instead bowed to the God of the Hebrew men. The rest is archived in history. But those were the giants of faith and very possibly paved the way and encouraged Daniel not much after, to stand against another despot King Darius – Daniel 6.

Bold in the face of threats by fire and the lions? That was indeed true boldness. That boldness was anchored in the unshakable faith of Meshach, Shadrach, Abednego and Daniel in their God. They had spiritual intimacy with that God and the inner assurance, conviction and direction from Him. Sure enough God made the giant out of the simple Hebrew men. They came to Babylon as slaves but rose to Prime Minister and Governors in the land.

Goliath may be big in body-mass but it was David that became the "real giant!" That's the character of true boldness.

Oh that God would give our world more people like Meshach, Shadrach, Abednego, Daniel, Jesus' disciples Peter and John [Acts 4:13], John Knox of England, Benson Idahosa of Africa, Billy Graham and other men and women of faith, told and untold, known and unknown, who will be bold enough to startle Kings and Presidents; men and women who like the Queen of Scotland in John Knox's time would fear their boldness and prayers "more than all the assembled armies of Europe."

Oh that God would give us giants–men and women who like those faith-worthies of Hebrews chapter 11, who through faith in God were made strong and emboldened; men and women who would refuse the allure and trappings of royalty, choosing instead to suffer affliction with God's people and by so doing subdued kingdoms, quenched violence of fire, stopped the mouths of lions, declaring that a better promise worth contending for lies ahead of those who would step out boldly and in faith.

DETRACTORS

As I look back to my growing years in management, I cannot forget some of the major catalysts to leadership along the way – for me. I was offered the challenging position in this fast growing conglomerate. The pay was good. So also was the prospect of advancing. I took the job anyway, against the counsel of a business friend who thought that the organization had a bad cultural reputation for "hiring and firing." Few months into my new job, we had a minor slip on the job. One of my subordinates had dropped the ball. Well, I was the boss and had responsibility for the actions and inactions of the department's folks. But again, in my mind's eye, the error was most inconsequential until it was magnified and attracted upper management's attention. A well respected colleague of mine swung by my office and asked to have a chat with me, least expecting it had anything to do with the issue that I considered rather trivial. But it was. My colleague whispered that the word making the rounds had it that I was incapable and might be asked to tender my resignation. Boy. Did it bother me that people were making a mountain out of a mole? You bet. Several days after, still bothered, I thought back to my business friend's counsel who warned against joining the organization because of their reputation for "hiring and firing." But soon enough, I reminded myself that I will not be detracted by the rumor mill. I continued my job and this time, had my house set in order. Weeks and months passed into becoming my first anniversary and I was still on the job! I stayed in that organization for twenty-eight years and retired not just as the Chief Executive, but as the Group Coordinator for the chain of businesses owned by the conglomerate.

What happened as I later found out was that a "nay-sayer" had reported what he did not see or hear or know anything about to his supervisor and of course, his supervisor still dazed by the acceptance of this new kid on the block, and moved with envy, reported to his own manager who thought it a duty to draw my boss's attention to what just happened. My boss thanked the reporter and sent him away. Management however gave me the benefit of the doubt for the error, being new on the job. As has most of the time been my response in such situation, I was determined more than ever before to do "whatsoever my hands finds to do" with excellence. I stayed focused and moving on boldly, not giving in to detractors, I was able to scale that hurdle – even though insignificant at the time–as I thought, to the shame of the envious colleague.

I should point out that couple of years later, I had the rarest privilege of being promoted ahead of not only the manager-reporter but several others my equal.

So the problem was obviously not with the organization's culture, rather it had to do with individual employees whose unrealistic expectations from a "big" company consigned them erroneously on the "entitlement" row.

There was a rather dramatic story told in I Kings chapter 13. This prophet from Judah was worshipping at the temple in Bethel where Israel's King Jeroboam was desecrating the altar at that same hour. Because it was contrary to the law that mandated only priests to sacrifice at such altars, the bold prophet pronounced God's judgment against the altar to the disdain of King Jeroboam. The King stretched his hand to order the prophet killed but his hand withered and would not go back to his body. That cowered the King's pride. He begged the prophet to pray for his hand's restoration. Yet in all of these, the prophet himself was never to bow to the palatial entreaties after the fulfillment of such divine mandate. Rather, he must return home some other way from how he came, not eating or drinking. The courage of the prophet from Judah was noised abroad until it gained national prominence. Presumably angered and somewhat ridiculed, an old prophet from Bethel was told about what the prophet from Judah did. He had a plan and the plan included detraction laced with deceit, so he could get the prophet from Judah detracted and possibly killed. He succeeded at both.

And the moral of the story? If you are convinced that the Lord gave you a mandate, you will do yourself a world of good to stay within that vision and to never allow detractors and distraction by whatever name and no matter how high or connected, take you off course.

So the problem was obviously not with the organization's culture, rather it had to do with individual employees whose unrealistic expectations from a "big" company consigned them erroneously on the "entitlement" row.

Be like the Apostle Paul, once he was convinced that the Lord had an assignment for him in Jerusalem, refused to be deterred even when a credible prophet Agabus along with others in Evangelist Philip's house seemed to be discouraging him from going. Here's how he responded to the seeming distraction:

> "And when he would not be persuaded, we ceased, saying, The will of the Lord be done"– Acts 21:8-14 [KJV]

That was how Paul overcame and fulfilled destiny: resistance through conviction.

That was how Nehemiah overcame – Nehemiah 6:1-13.

It turned out it was the same way Jesus overcame – Luke 4:1-13.

That was how Jesus' disciples and heroes of faith in Hebrews chapter 11 overcame.

That's how we will overcome: resistance over detractors and distractions through conviction! And that only comes by way of bravery and courage.

I suppose that most of my readers may have listened to or been told about the inspiring "If I had sneezed" speech by Dr. Martin Luther King. If you have not, I encourage you to go on the YouTube to check it out. That was a perfect story of distraction. In the story told by Dr. King himself, in the midst of going about doing what he felt called to do, a lady cornered him at a book signing and stabbed him, hoping he would die. But by heeding the medical personnel's advice never to sneeze at that crucial time that it made the difference, Dr. King survived when all that his detractors and their cronies wanted was to have him killed, so he does not fulfill destiny. Dr. King lived years after that to fulfill his mandate.

It is rather over-simplified I suppose, to think that one of the presumed attractions of success is criticism that most often leads to mere distraction – if not overcome by conviction. Detractors are often irked by your determination to break ranks.

MEN PLEASERS

On the flip side of people standing up against detractors are those that are preoccupied with wanting to please others.

While the bold, brave and courageous will not be detracted by flatteries and are ready to displease if need be, men pleasers get satisfaction from being praised – many times undeservedly. The bold do it for others; men pleasers do it for self. The bold are not afraid to be criticized; men pleasers get angered, nay threatened, by opposing views.

You probably have heard the story of the "little" king from the inconspicuous kingdom. He was the personification of bravery, courage and boldness. From his little corner, he had done so many things considered humanly near impossible for the betterment of his people. His fame astounded the neighboring "big" and so much more well-known king who felt threatened by the popularity of this little king and the proximity to his kingdom. His fear? Some day, the little-known king might have an ambition to annex his kingdom. Well, that was a mere illusion; but still…

One day, the bigger king summoned his council and organized the capture of the little king who, by the way, offered no serious military resistance. The little king was brought to the large kingdom and after series of interrogation which did not yield any substantive hint as to the secret of his prominence, had to be put to a public test, considered a ridicule, following which if he failed, was to be hung on the gallows.

His test was to carry a wide-seamed glass of water across the rocky mile long highway leading to the palace and back. Wherever he spilled the water was where he was to be hung.

To the utter amazement of the big king, the foe went and returned without spilling a drop. When he was asked the secret he told the king: "Long may you reign your majesty. As I went along the journey, I determined to not listen to the jeers on my left nor the praise on my right. I was not there to please either side. It was my journey of life. I felt lonely all through. And unless I was bold and determined enough to be above the jeers and the praises, I could never have made it." That seemed to be all that the bigger king needed.

He admired the wisdom and sincerity of the smaller king. And even though he would normally not have set the little opponent free, he was convinced that he had what he so much desired: to be bold even in the face of loneliness and never to be men-pleaser.

Men pleasers respond to criticism with a fight and flight. Bold people listen; take correction if, when and where needed to make themselves better. Men pleasers consider critics enemies. Bold people know that critics make them stronger and better and are necessary catalysts to enduring leadership. That was the case with King David and Paul's relative – Shimei in II Samuel 16 vv. 5 – 14. The Bible recorded for our wise counsel that because David neglected to respond negatively to the jeers of Shimei, he was able to arrive at his destination and was "refreshed."

Men pleasers would avoid ruffling feathers for the fear that they might be displaced. Bold people would stand their ground and be ready for the change even if it meant ruffling feathers.

Daniel, Meschach, Shadrack and Abednego were Hebrew men brought into Babylon as slaves. But because they chose to not be men-pleasers but rather acknowledge their God over the Babylonian monarchy, they became leaders and rulers over prominent indigenous others.

Stand up and stand out for what you belief. Stay bold and never give in to distractions: the jeers and praises – no matter how credible or incredible they seem. Paying undue attention to criticism simply makes you miserable. Getting engrossed in praise simply makes you sycophant.

Remember, your success does not necessarily depend on the happiness or otherwise of others. It depends on you knowing and doing what you believe God is calling you to do at a particular time, situation and place. So, realize that you will always have both sets of people: the happy-campers and critics around you – unless of course you do nothing. You will always have that impossible-to-please skeptic and the presumed-devotee. To the one: nothing that you do will be good enough – be it around where you live, work or even at Church. To the other: nothing that you do can be wrong – most often if it enhances their ego and makes them get their wishes from you.

How about measuring these two groups by their relevance: whether or not they care enough to get you to fulfill your dream? If they don't, they are at best distraction. Avoid them.

You are not men-pleaser. You are not moved by flattery. You are not out to impress or entertain. Rather, you are on your way to leadership. You cannot be distracted.

BULLIES

Bullies are detractors of a different kind. They want you to believe how they are stronger than you; bigger than you; richer than you; more influential and connected than you. It is the intention of a bully to hurt you quite alright, but most times, a bully wants you to surrender what you have and subject you to a perpetual fear of them so you could be subservient and continually perceive them as more important than they really are.

It is most common that you identify the bully among school mates but beyond schools, bullies abound in businesses as in religious groups and governments. Nomenclature may change but the motives and characteristics remain: repulsive desire to lord it over others.

In my primary school days, school mate Josh was often bullied by this "small devil" so-called – Sam.

Sam gnaws at and beats Josh every time their paths crossed.

Josh prayed and made frantic efforts everyday to never cross paths with Sam. Anytime Sam accosted Josh, the only escape was to appease Sam with his snacks which Josh's poor mom packs for him since they do not have enough money for him always to buy snacks at school. Even though their classrooms were on different blocks, somehow they unavoidably meet at corridors or cafeteria few times. You guessed right what happened at such times: Sam bullies and Josh surrenders his snacks. Co-students would chuckle and get the kicker out of the scenario. Some of them would even tell the Josh-Sam debacle to their parents until Josh's dad, many months later heard. Josh's dad was going to go to the school, report what he had been told, so that the authorities would investigate. But little Josh profusely begged his dad not to; because it would worsen the situation and might lead to being ostracized by his peers. "Well" said the dad, "then you must do something on your own to stop it or I'll go over there." Of course the boy agreed, only that his little frame was no match for the bigger and taller Sam–the bully. It all continued until it peaked this summer day. Josh came back scratched, beaten and hungry. By this time, the dad was determined to go but he realized that his son could very possibly get into more troubles. So he thought of what to do.

He asked little Josh how many hands Sam has? "Two" he replied. "And you?" Josh replied "Two also dad." "How many eyes does Sam have?" the dad asked. "Two" said Josh. "And you?" the dad asked. "Two dad" he replied. "How many heads does Sam have?" the dad asked yet again. "One" said Josh. "And you?" "One dad" he replied. "So now I want you to go back to that "..." and when next he confronts you, give him a piece of action." By that the dad meant, resist him. Initially, it didn't work because Josh lived under the fear he might only aggravate things. Finally, unknown to anyone including Josh's dad, he determined that he had had enough of Sam's intimidation and would have none of it going forward. He had his snack packed and made up his mind he was going to be the one to eat it that day and no longer Sam. Bully Sam saw Josh coming to school that morning with his lunch bag and began to scheme how he was going to catch up with Josh for a treat except that this very day was different.

Sam watched from distance as Josh moved out of class and followed after him. He picked the fight as always, but this time, Josh reassured himself it was going to be the last fight. He dropped his lunch bag aside, pulled off his sandals and opened his eyes as if to make a bold declaration: "You have made me miserable long enough" he yelled at Sam. "Back off or I'll tell you who I truly am." In a fist of sudden rage, Josh rushed at Sam, pushed him and to his utter surprise, down went Sam. "Really?" he thought to himself. And even though Sam had only tripped, Josh took advantage of his fall nonetheless, went over Sam and not giving him any breather, began to punch and to kick so hard, it attracted the school. Sam was ashamed, no, he was humiliated, that little Josh would fight and over-power him. But true to Josh, it was the last fight; the deciding fight; the bold fight. It was the determination to put an end to years of intimidation. He did. He won and lived peacefully ever thereafter. The two boys became friends many years after when they both had left school and continued to lightly made mockery of themselves. Josh saved himself by taking the risk, being brave and moving boldly.

How about principalities? Them too.

Christians experience principalities. And like youngster bullies, principalities will resist and attempt to subdue you until, if allowed, they render you and your vision ineffective.

You could not have forgotten the Bible story of Pharaoh who as slaves owner over the children of Israel many years ago attempted to scuttle God's divine plan for their deliverance.

Not until the coming of Moses and the harsh realities of the Passover would he let Israel go – Exodus chapters 5 to 14.

King Ahasuerus, that notable ruler of ancient Persia, Media, and Babylonia was not so much of a bully as his high chief Haman. You'll find the account of Haman's oppression in the book of Esther chapters 3 to 8. Haman would not sleep until the bold and determined Mordecai and his fellow Jews were wasted. He schemed before the King to have them killed. But God's plan has always been different. Bold Esther would go before the King – even at the risk of her life, in order to dis-annul Haman's game-plan. Of course, she did not die. Neither did Mordecai and the Jews.

The answer is always to be bold and to never allow bullies, principalities, powers or spiritual wickedness intimidate you.

Be ready to take risks. Be brave. Be courageous. Be bold.

It was Charlotte Elliott [1789-1871] who I suppose may very possibly have experienced what I am talking about in her hymn "Watch & Pray." In one of the stanzas, she stated:

"Principalities and powers,
Mustering their unseen array,
Wait for thy unguarded hours:
Watch and pray."

We all certainly are in the midst of ambushed foes and undoubtedly need to gird our heavenly armor on – day and night.

OBSESSIVE COMPULSIVENESS

What boldness is not.

It perhaps looks like it, but it is not. Rather obsessive compulsiveness is boldness stripped of reasoning and direction.

Boldness goes beyond bold-face. It is not the dismissal of a situation as non-existent or the looking down on contemporaries, or anyone for that matter – in arrogance or with ridicule.

Whereas the obsessive compulsive person just wants it done – whether or not it adds to objectives, provided it alleviates his/her anxiety, a bold rationale person gives serious thought to why it has to be done – usually for the promotion and betterment of a cause.

While this must not by any means be taken to underplay the seriousness of the scientific discoveries in obsessive compulsive personality disorders or over-simplify its effects; it nonetheless highlights the dangers of preoccupation with logic and intellect, to the exclusion of relevance. It is to point out the erroneous deference accorded it to the extent that it has in many cases, been equated to conscientiousness.

In my working years, I have found personalities with obsessive compulsiveness to believe that they function best when they are in the "power" and "control" modes. Everyone around them cannot be right unless they defer to them and do things their way.

Unfortunately though, obsessive compulsive individuals feel uncomfortable and somewhat threatened in the presence of others that appear to know better or do things better than them.

Obsessive compulsive person is the least conscientious. Many times, it has been the excuse not to do anything. At best, obsessive compulsive individuals are abrasive, irrationally self-centered and inflexible. They are blind-sighted and want things done their way and at any cost – without thinking of the cost-benefit or the resultant consequences.

This, unfortunately cannot be the right "determined difference" but rather a gambling chance of "do-it-or-else..." pervasive syndrome.

This is more true in the light of Jesus' admonition:

> "...don't begin until you count the cost. For who would begin construction of a building without

first calculating the cost to see if there is enough money to finish it? Otherwise, you might complete only the foundation before running out of money, and then everyone would laugh at you. They would say, 'There's the person who started that building and couldn't afford to finish it!' "Or what king would go to war against another king without first sitting down with his counselors to discuss whether his army of 10,000 could defeat the 20,000 soldiers marching against him? And if he can't, he will send a delegation to discuss terms of peace while the enemy is still far away. So you cannot become my disciple without giving up everything you own."– Luke 14:28-33 [NLT]

Christians desiring to take on leadership roles have the responsibility to check their lives for obsessive compulsive tendencies and to repent, asking the Lord for help in balancing their thoughts and actions.

While our world is waiting for the manifestation of the sons and daughters of God, it behooves true Christ's ambassadors to know the people around them and their needs–so as to offer impulsive-free, yet determined, bold and courageous help to a needing, hurtful world.

More than anyone else and any time before, the sheep today need true lessons on boldness that is void of obsessive compulsiveness.

INPUDENCE

Impudence is the other side of boldness that is offensive. Coming from the Latin *im* – meaning without and *pudens* meaning shame, impudence is disrespectful and shameless.

Boldness might be the other side of the "shy" coin quite alright, but it is never conceited, cocky, egotistical or impudent. It is never contemptuous or bad-mannered. It does not vaunt youthful exuberance in the face of elders.

An aspiring leader understands that...

"The glory of the young is their strength; *but* the gray hair of experience is the splendor of the old."–Proverbs 20:29 [NLT]

and takes seriously the admonition...

"...Likewise, you who are younger, be subject to the elders. Clothe yourselves, all of you, with humility toward one another, for "God opposes the proud but gives grace to the humble." – I Peter 5:5 [ESV]

When a generation turns impudent, it manifests in failing to recognize the gray hair and hoary head, it then begins to nullify God's Word and slide into disobedience and lawlessness [Matthew 15:5-9]. It becomes prejudicial and despises the wisdom of elders. Impudence reveres brute force and vulgarity. Thus an aspiring leader is denied necessary baton of experience from their forebears.

Such was the nature of impudence when Israel's King Rehoboam succeeded in fragmenting an otherwise peaceful nation because he despised the counsel of his elders. He suffered the disintegration of order and not only did the people leave the united kingdom over which he reigned, they also left him – I Kings 12:1-20.

But it was not so when God gave their forebears the principles of realizing sustainable leadership – individually as well as communally –

"For I have chosen him, so that he will direct his children and his household after him to keep the way of the LORD by doing what is right and just, so that the LORD will bring about for Abraham what he has promised him" – Genesis 18:19 [NIV]

Today, it continues to be true that a people that undermines the influence and guidance of the elderly cannot but be impudent and prone to straying from the path of sustainable growth. Any wonder why we have no lack of mediocres in places where matured and enduring leadership are most needed?

Mike Dowgiewicz of the Hebraic Foundations[2] told a story in one of their articles on impudence that I thought very aptly captures the lesson on playing the "impudent":

> "In Africa 20 years ago, the National Park Service was faced with a ruinous overpopulation of elephants. To keep the animals from plundering valuable crops and defoliating the land, naturalists killed all the adult elephants, preserving only the young. As these youngsters matured, the male calves in particular grew violent, attacking and killing both rhinos and people. Their fierce, aggressive behavior was totally out of character. It was as though the restraint common to elephants had vanished — or had never developed. The park naturalists were clueless as to who or what was responsible for attacking and killing so many rhinos. At first they blamed poachers. That still left unexplained, however, the vicious attacks on humans in the area. When they finally discovered that the havoc was being caused by the young elephants, the rangers moved quickly. Each misbehaving elephant was issued a "rap sheet" similar to that of a street criminal to identify those with aggressive behavior. When a particular elephant accumulated too many points against his behavior, he was destroyed. But that didn't solve the real underlying problem. Many hours of study later, the naturalists realized that male elephants, young ones especially, have such high testosterone levels that they need the restraining behavior of older elephant males to keep them in control. It was

the mature males who taught the young to spar with one another to relieve their sexual tension. In essence, the older males taught the junior elephants a pecking order of deference. Desperate to restore order to this unruly community of young males, the naturalists imported adult males into the herd. Not long after, deference was established and more orderly behavior restored."

That was said to be in Africa 20 odd years ago. It very much looks like we have traces of this same type behavior in today's developed world and I submit that it begs Christian managers to the rescue.

Any wonder why we have no lack of mediocres in places where matured and enduring leadership are most needed?

CERTAINLY NOT FOR THE FAINT-HEARTED

Most cultures celebrate rites of passage. Arguably the most intriguing of the rites is the passage from adolescent to adulthood. And unlike the western ideology of "leaving it to chance," the rite gives adolescents rare privilege of knowing how to face life's challenges that they are bound to face. The rites are performed by the community elders and experienced mentors. The ceremonies could include some form of initiation and/or psy-op, mainly aimed at letting the youngster know that s/he no longer should succumb to life's challenges nor be frightened by environmental scares. They are taught how to bring down oppositions and to overcome aggressor's intimidation: be they from humans or animals. They are made aware that those that will become leaders of the communities must not only be known to be strong – physically and emotionally, but that they also must show bravery.

Initiation rites might involve being kept away several days in a relatively lonely environment, denied of accustomed convenience and reliance. Initiates are made to feel the pains of suffering – all in order to instill tenacity, endurance, fearlessness and readiness for that stage of life.

In some cultures, the rite of passage takes few days and in others months. Should an initiate fail an initial test, he may be kept longer in deprivation or given some other form of laborious test until he begins to harden up and made ready to face life's challenges.

It is just another way of the community passing on to the up-coming generations the lesson that life and the coming of age must not be taken for granted and that the faint-hearted cannot and will not succeed in the myriad of life's issues.

If the un-Christian world understands that enduring leadership requires unusual bravery and audacity, and makes such elaborate efforts in preparing up and coming generations for the passage into it, it becomes baffling why Christians who are supposed to be leading the world should not know nor appreciate.

Back in the Bible Old Testament Book of Judges, one of Israel's judges was confronted by neighboring enemies. The Midianites attacked Israel so hard and for so long until Gideon took the challenge and decided to call their bluff. He was assured of God to go against them. But then he needed support soldiers and he gathered thirty-two thousand. But it was a paltry three hundred of these many thousands that would follow Gideon to war. These were people who have learnt to be vigilant, brave and ready to fight at an instant.

Read Judges 7:1-8

Read the description of David's followers while he was running from his erstwhile boss – King Saul, in first Chronicles 12:1-15 and you will be amazed at the hardness of his highly trained companions-bodyguards:

- armed men who were able to shoot arrows or to sling stones right-handed or left-handed,
- brave warriors,
- men that were ready for battle and able to handle the shield and spear,
- men whose faces were the faces of lions,
- men that were as swift as gazelles in the mountains

- the least of the men was able to put a hundred to flight
- the greatest of them was able to drive away a thousand.

Those were no sissies. They were no cry-babies nor were they faint-hearted.

It is no surprise that it took the disciples of Jesus Christ more than three years to get the lesson on enduring leadership through pains. On one such lesson, Jesus rebuked their fear:

> "And when he was entered into a ship, his disciples followed him. And, behold, there arose a great tempest in the sea, insomuch that the ship was covered with the waves: but he was asleep. And his disciples came to him, and awoke him, saying, Lord, save us: we perish. And he saith unto them, Why are ye fearful, O ye of little faith? Then he arose, and rebuked the winds and the sea; and there was a great calm. But the men marvelled, saying, What manner of man is this, that even the winds and the sea obey him!"
> Matthew 8:23-27 [KJV]

Those were no sissies. They were no cry-babies nor were they faint-hearted.

Thank God for spiritual adoption and the rite of Christian passage. Thank God that we have not received the spirit of fear but of boldness and bravery.–Romans 8:14-15

BOLDNESS FACTORS

Most often than not, consciously or otherwise, we all stop to question what or who may be behind the bold person's guts. Politicians are quick to want to discover the invisible hands and motives of their bold opponents. They try to unearth the weight, the strength and severity of this boldness; these all, with the intention of coming up with commensurate strategy/ies to overcome or at the very least resist it.

Like as in human relationships, boldness produced as a result of knowing and taking advantage of the partner's weakness is in many instances staged, producing subjective consequences.

On the other hand, innate gift of boldness, even though tending towards being provocative, is daring, fearless and most often conspicuous.

Notwithstanding, boldness without corresponding influencing accompaniment is soon silenced and discouraged.

There is the third aspect of boldness that has a marked definitive difference. It is the Christ-centered boldness. It is courage at its core. It is the boldness that enables determined difference.

By the way, this type-courage expresses itself at the mid-way of two extremes:

i.   Not doing or saying anything about our convictions which is tantamount to being a **coward** and

ii. Rushing to do or say too much which translates to **foolishness**

It is possible to not be innately bold, but the knowledge of Jesus Christ and what He has done in our lives gives us the courage and boldness to assure others He can do the same for them. It is what motivates our love and compassion for others and tempered with integrity, have the surpassing power to break down barriers and to say and do what needed said and/or done, thus making a determined difference.

Interestingly, these factors are *never superficial* or *staged*. They come with close relationship to the Lord, understanding who we truly are in the Lord and taking the tenets of our faith seriously enough that they manifest on the outside.

That was the kind of courage Abishai – one of the major commanders of David's army had. You could read his many exploits in 1st and 2nd Samuel as well as in the Book of Chronicles. Together with his thirty or so colleagues, principal amongst whom were Benaiah and Asazel, did what could otherwise be considered humanly impossible.

Even though a strong and bold soldier in his own right, he remained *submissive* to the leadership of David. He was *trusted* enough to go down with David into Saul's camp where he took Saul's spear and cruse at his bolster – I Samuel 26:6-12; he broke through the Philistine's army to fetch water meant to quench David's thirst – II Samuel 23:13-16 and with his undisguised *loyalty* to David defended him against eighteen thousand Edomites that he slew – I Chronicles 18:12-13. That was determined difference.

The accounts of Daniel, Shadrach, Meshach and Abednego recorded in the Book of Daniel are replete with examples of making the determined difference through their bold faith. It remains a classic history, yet prophetic messages for those who desire to make the difference by their *faith*.

The Jewish local government counselor Joseph of Arimathea was described as "honorable," and "waiting for the Kingdom of God." But the most attractive and relevant description of this man was the fact that he was "bold" to approach Pilate for the body of Jesus – Mark 15:43.

This is boldness that would not be bothered by what peers think. It is boldness that would not consider political correctness. It is boldness that defies stigma. Disgrace, dishonor and humiliation cannot withstand it. That was the boldness Paul had and described in his First Thessalonians epistle [2:1-2].

That was the characteristics of the boldness of the Early Church. They *prayed* for it.

In their case, boldness came through *intimacy* with the Lord.

Could you imagine how the ministry of unlearned Peter and John in the Book of the Acts of the Apostles 4:1-31 confounded the entire city, their priests, the Sadducees and the captain of the Jerusalem temple? The Scriptures record that...

"Now when they saw the *boldness* of Peter and John, and perceived that they were unlearned and ignorant men, they marveled; and they took knowledge of them, that *they had been with Jesus*" – Acts 4:13 [KJV]

Peter and John did not stop there. They also encouraged the Body of Believers [vv. 23-31] to join in praying for boldness! Would you?

Proverbs 28:1 says it all…

"The wicked flee when no man pursues, but the righteous are as *bold* as a lion." [KJ2]

Amos 3:3 also says…

"Can two people walk together without agreeing on the direction?" [NLT]

Boldness is *never superficial* or *staged*
Boldness is *submissive* and *trustworthy*
Boldness is *loyal*
Boldness defies *stigma*
These are what distinguish the innate gift of boldness from that which is spiritually-backed.

This is boldness that would not be bothered by what peers think.
It is boldness that would not consider political correctness.
It is boldness that defies stigma.

But principally… boldness that would make an enduring difference comes through intimacy with the Divine and in a righteous walk with the Lord.

Ephesians 3:12…
"In whom [Jesus] we have boldness and access with confidence by the faith of him." [KJV]

Hebrews 4:16…
"Let us therefore come boldly unto the throne of grace, that we may obtain mercy, and find grace to help in time of need." [KJV]

Hebrews 10:19-23...

"Having therefore, brethren, boldness to enter into the holiest by the blood of Jesus, by a new and living way, which he hath consecrated for us, through the veil, that is to say, his flesh; And *having* an high priest over the house of God; Let us draw near with a true heart in full assurance of faith, having our hearts sprinkled from an evil conscience, and our bodies washed with pure water. Let us hold fast the profession of *our* faith without wavering; (for he *is* faithful that promised;)" [KJV]

References:
[1] LBD Apparel–Pedro Pertile and Camaren Walker
[2] Elephants Without Deference–Restoration Ministries International; www.restorationministries.org

PRINCIPLE FIVE

Determine... to Stay Focused:

Set attention on your object [your goal] among many
lookalikes or even differing, distracting objects.
"Give whatever you are doing and whoever you are
with the gift of your attention." [1]–Jim Rohn

"Above all else, guard your heart, for everything
you do flows from it. Keep your mouth free of
perversity; keep corrupt talk far from your lips.
Let your eyes look straight ahead; fix your gaze
directly before you. Give careful thought to the
paths for your feet and be steadfast in all your
ways. Do not turn to the right or the left; keep
your foot from evil."–Proverbs 4:23-27 [NIV]

STAY
FOCUSED!

FOCUS...

This is the act of paying particular attention to; concentrating on, zeroing in on some important matter to the exclusion of matters of less importance.

Here's what the Apostle preached to his followers on the subject of focus:

> "Brethren, I count not myself to have apprehended: but this one thing I do, forgetting those things which are behind, and reaching forth unto those things which are before, I press toward the mark for the prize of the high calling of God in Christ Jesus." Philippians 3:13-14 [KJV]

Here are his basics of focus:
1. do not think your past achievement the ultimate: you could improve
2. do not get unreasonably carried away by past achievement: stay humble
3. discover what it is you are called to do: that is God's calling upon your life
4. continue at it: stay focused and work to the best of your ability

That is not to say that your past has nothing to do with your present and future.

Your past is what brought you where you are at. Without the elements of your past, you could not be at your present and your future could neither be guaranteed.

Your past could very well be the motivation and launching pad to the opportunities of the present and future.

The important thing is to realize that your past was limited. You now hold limitless potential in the present and future that is waiting to be expressed through determined yet thoughtful focus.

In life's journey that's filled with a lot more of mere activities and little of realities, the rat race produces little of achievers and more of activists. It produces severe and uneasy inequality among the haves and have-nots.

We get easily distracted, chasing shadows, overwhelmed, stressed and spread too thin till we lose focus on substance and redefine limits to exclude boundaries. Worse still is the fact that the danger signals are most often ignored in our activity trappings.

Remember the allegoric story of the "busy" watchman in I Kings 20:35-43?

Right at the battlefield, an enemy combatant was caught and kept in the custody of this watchman. But alas, the watchman was busy "here and there" so much that the combatant escaped from under his no-watch nay, no-focus. The metaphoric judgment as consequence did not seem pleasant some three thousand years ago, neither is it today:

> "'Guard this man. If he is missing, it will be your life for his life, or you must pay a talent of silver.' While your servant was busy here and there, the man disappeared." "That is your sentence," the king of Israel said. "You have pronounced it yourself." – I Kings 20:39-40 [NIV]

Penalty of death in exchange for the life of the escapee or some hefty ransom? How so severe? But that, inadvertently, has always been the price of distraction!

We get easily distracted, chasing shadows, overwhelmed, stressed and spread too thin till we lose focus on substance and redefine limits to exclude boundaries.

If the recent Credit Suisse's Report[2] is anything to go by, it is obvious that we have a rather unfair spread of global wealth where the world's top 1% owns about 50% of the world's wealth while conversely 1% of the world's wealth is owned by the bottom 50%.

Could it be that only the top 1% of the world's population truly understands the concept of focusing on their interest better than the rest: discovering what is most important in their lives and are pursuing it? After all, as we understand from the Scriptures, opportunities are available to all:

> "... the race is not to the swift or the battle to the strong, nor does food come to the wise or wealth to the brilliant or favor to the learned; but time and chance happen to them all." – Ecclesiastes 9:11 [NIV]

It really should not be the exclusive privilege of the few. Opportunities abound for each of us. It just turns out that what we look at and glib over without paying enough close attention as in focusing, becomes the treasure of immense value in the hands of the man and woman who chose to focus.

That was true of the likes of Italian sculptor-painter Michelangelo di Lodovico Buonarroti Simoni [1475-1564]; the likes of Leonardo da Vinci [1452-1519] and it still holds true today. While the 99% saw garbage and many times what they thought were illusions and paid no attention, these stopped, saw through the rubbish so called, observed, concentrated attention and it wasn't too long that they produced something unbelievably valuable and enduring. The power of focus.

If I have any amount of focus, it was because I have a wife whose song was simply "focus." She better understands what it means to focus when she constantly reminds me to concentrate on primary subject to the exclusion of irrelevants and distractions.

Now I know experientially that the Spanish philosopher Jose Ortega y Gasset [1883-1955] could not be wrong when he said:

> "Tell me to what you pay attention and I will tell you who you are."

I also constantly remind myself that Joseph the dreamer in the Bible was a man of tremendous focus. He had brutal trials that very well passed as distractions many times: planned against, jeered at, thrown into the pit to die, reported as dead but sold as slave, suffered servitude pains, ridiculed, falsely accused, imprisoned and forgotten and disappointed by those he thought should help him in the time of his need when he had previously helped these. But in all these he refused to give in or give up. Rather, he stayed the course. He kept focus of his dream. He believed that if God ordained him as leader that he saw in the twice revealed dream, it was his responsibility to stay focused. His fascinating story as told in Genesis 37 through 41 is a must-read to aspiring Christian leaders.

So was Moses. We are told that:

> "...when he grew up, refused to be called the son of Pharaoh's daughter. He chose to share the oppression of God's people instead of enjoying the fleeting pleasures of sin. He thought it was better to suffer for the sake of Christ than to own the treasures of Egypt, for he was looking ahead to his great reward. It was by faith that Moses left the land of Egypt, not fearing the king's anger. He kept right on going because he kept his eyes on the one who is invisible." – Hebrews 11:24-27 [NLT]

There were others that made a distinctive difference:

> "...of Gideon, Barak, Samson, Jephthah, David, Samuel, and all the prophets; these people overthrew kingdoms, ruled with justice, and received what God had promised them. They shut the mouths of lions, quenched the flames of fire, and escaped death by the edge of the sword. Their weakness was turned to strength. They became strong in battle and put whole armies to flight.

Women received their loved ones back again from death. But others were tortured, refusing to turn from God in order to be set free. They placed their hope in a better life after the resurrection. Some were jeered at, and their backs were cut open with whips. Others were chained in prisons. Some died by stoning, some were sawed in half, and others were killed with the sword. Some went about wearing skins of sheep and goats, destitute and oppressed and mistreated. They were too good for this world, wandering over deserts and mountains, hiding in caves and holes in the ground. All these people earned a good reputation because of their faith, yet none of them received all that God had promised." – Hebrews 11:32-39 [NLT]

These men and women had a choice to jump ship in the face of trials but no. They focused their attention on what they believed were their set mandates. They refused to let go. They refused to "curse God and die." They were not ashamed of their God. They considered all else non-essential. And as foreigners and nomads, they believed and so set their focus, their attention and longing on some distant promised country that is better than where they came from: a city whose architect and builder is God.

But in all these he refused to give in or give up. Rather, he stayed the course. He kept focus of his dream. He believed that if God ordained him as leader that he saw in the twice revealed dream, it was his responsibility to stay focused.

Their faces were set ahead of them and not looking back, they stayed the course and won their races and fulfilled destiny. That, my friend, is true focus.

Now I see why God would create the face looking forward instead of looking backward: so we could stay focused on the things that lie ahead instead of reminiscing on past glory or failure.

Could it be that we all, with the exception of the 1% of course, need a reorientation of our mindset in the area of focusing: perhaps a better understanding of what it is and how we could best apply it to our daily living?

IDENTITY

Focus is simply about reflecting and paying attention to the things that are around you in order to identify what's important among several other look-alikes or distractions. It is the ability to reflect and concentrate on what you had your mind set to achieve from the onset–despite distractions: what you need to get to where you determine to get. That sounds more like focus to me. It is.

I couldn't ever forget the lesson on "spotting the difference" that I learnt as a teenager in the primary school. The soccer coach had three identical balls for our class' friendly match with the other class. He showed us the real ball that we were allowed to score with but since it was a lesson on staying focused, he let us know that the other two balls will simultaneously be on the field. We could kick and pass any of the balls but only the "real" play-ball was accepted for a score. It was the responsibility of both teams to watch the ball that we kick through the goals on either side. It turned out that both teams, in the frantic bid to win over the other, really had a zero draw game. No one scored with the right ball! The seeming score by our opponents was disqualified because of being offside. Quite interesting you would imagine but how so true of life's events. We all, most of the time focus on scoring over others that we lose the rule of the game.

If we had paid more attention to identifying what we are playing with: the object at stake and how we are playing: the issues at stake; how so much more successful we all would be in the game of life?

Today, I understand Paul's admonition better when he said in I Corinthians 9:24-27 [NIV]:

"Do you not know that in a race all the runners run, but only one gets the prize? Run in such a way as to get the prize. Everyone who competes in the games goes into strict training. They do it to get a crown that will not last, but we do it to get a crown that will last forever. Therefore I do not run like someone running aimlessly; I do not fight like a boxer beating the air. No, I strike a blow to my body and make it my slave so that after I have preached to others, I myself will not be disqualified for the prize."

The athlete's one important lesson to-keep is of necessity staying focused in the field of play, when every move though similar to prior ones, are different, requiring more specific style and strategy.

We cannot allow the look-alikes of life, the different shades of grey and the games of chance sway us from our planned goal, even when others seem convinced that such look-alikes are missed opportunities. We know otherwise that they actually are not but mere distraction. Amen.

Identify what it is you are called to do. Stay focused to do it and leave the rest to the One that called and mandated you.

Yeap. Focus is all about identity. It is giving meaning to your personality.

The athlete's one important lesson to-keep is of necessity staying focused in the field of play, when every move though similar to prior ones, are different, requiring more specific style and strategy.

HOARDERS and CLUTTER

From children's toys that were once useful and relevant to big boys' toys that litter the rooms and spaces in the house – even when there have been no real need for them, most of us do have some amount of clutter. These often prevent us from knowing or seeing what is in vogue, relevant and worth keeping. They prevent us from paying attention where we should. It just turned out that these add needless costs to our already strained budget.

Once in a while, how about stopping around the room or office space to check the relevance of the items lying around before we turn the space into mad man's chamber? Perhaps a needed yard sale?

Just as with objects, so with thoughts and actions: we fill our minds with so many distractions and wonder why we do not seem to be making any significant difference in what we do.

We get easily sidetracked into redundant affairs just for momentary satisfaction – most times without realizing it.

We have favorite shows and spend so much time in front of the television.

We read comics for the sake of stimulation and are proud we kept the primary editions, even when they have turned dusty heap.

We engage quality time in activities not directly related to our set-goals and little or no time on what really matters.

Hoarders we all.

I love Paul's three-way test of de-cluttering: Is it right? Is it beneficial? Is it expedient?–1 Corinthians 6:12. It is another way of asking ourselves whether or not what we hold dear is appropriate, valuable and prudent. Instead of blinding ourselves with the clutter of busy-ness and mere activity, it is in defining why we need to do what we do or want to do.

Would to God that we set boundaries and stick with it longer: that we know, choose and focus on what is right, beneficial and expedient.

LOSING IT

Fifteen hundred years before Christ, ancient Egypt was the world's super power. The Pharaohs were the semi-gods of their time. Their influence extended far and wide in the now Middle East; and the nation of Egypt had what could be regarded as one of the world's earliest civilizations. They prided themselves in science and economics and know the dynamics of human endeavors.

You will remember that the Jews were in bondage under Egypt by God's design and by Egypt's cruelty, whatever they commanded the Jews to do they obeyed until Israel's cries caught God's attention.

My take in this story was the fact that in order to get the Jews serve with undivided attention, Egypt assessed their labor and increased it from time to time. First, they had them go bring clay that was used in producing bricks supposedly from distant places; then they added fetching of the water required for tempering the clay. And as if those were not enough, they had them travel far and wide to bring straws for strengthening the bricks and after that, scarce stubbles instead of straws – all in the bid to afflict the Jews with heavy burdens and so make them *lose* the focus of ever thinking of self development or escaping from the shackles of slavery but rather to keep them as slaves perpetually. That story could be found in Exodus 1:8-14 and 5:6-14.

Ordinarily, you don't think much of this strategy except that it was painful on the Jews, until you bring it to today's application and the consequences of not focusing.

You make money and desire what the Jones' have. But your budget does not allow it. So you voluntarily demand "more labor," "more on-duty hours." You take on the second job and sometimes the third–in the bid to afford the "toy." You are even encouraged to cover what was excess uncovered by credit card and unbeknown to you, subtly but surely, there came the resulting aggravation of financial burden, the pressure of work – including at nights and weekends, the emotional distraught, the clutter that follows and finally, the loss of focus on what should be important. Same tactic, same result. Give them more work so they don't or rather can't focus.

Do you wonder how well-meaning Christians with good intentions slide into a state of spiritual coldness and not long after if not checked, lose the faith?

Beware of distractions: you could lose what's important to you!

…your budget does not allow it. So you voluntarily demand "more labor," "more on-duty hours." You take on the second job and sometimes the third–in the bid to afford the "toy."

DON'T GET ENTANGLED

There are two Bible parables that I find very fascinating in studying the matter of focus. Both parables teach profound lessons on not getting entangled, as remedy for distraction:

The first parable is from Jesus' very popular Sermon on the Mount:

> "Do not store up for yourselves treasures on earth, where moths and vermin destroy, and where thieves break in and steal. But store up for yourselves treasures in heaven, where moths and vermin do not destroy, and where thieves do not break in and steal. For where your treasure is, there your heart will be also.

> "The eye is the lamp of the body. If your eyes are healthy your whole body will be full of light. But if your eyes are unhealthy, your whole body will be full of darkness. If then the light within you is darkness, how great is that darkness!

"No one can serve two masters. Either you will hate the one and love the other, or you will be devoted to the one and despise the other. You cannot serve both God and money.

"Therefore I tell you, do not worry about your life, what you will eat or drink; or about your body, what you will wear. Is not life more than food, and the body more than clothes? Look at the birds of the air; they do not sow or reap or store away in barns, and yet your heavenly Father feeds them. Are you not much more valuable than they? Can any one of you by worrying add a single hour to your life?

"And why do you worry about clothes? See how the flowers of the field grow. They do not labor or spin. Yet I tell you that not even Solomon in all his splendor was dressed like one of these. If that is how God clothes the grass of the field, which is here today and tomorrow is thrown into the fire, will he not much more clothe you — you of little faith? So do not worry, saying, 'What shall we eat?' or 'What shall we drink?' or 'What shall we wear?' For the pagans run after all these things, and your heavenly Father knows that you need them. But seek first his kingdom and his righteousness, and all these things will be given to you as well. Therefore do not worry about tomorrow, for tomorrow will worry about itself. Each day has enough trouble of its own-Matthew 6:19-34 [NIV]

There are three parts to this parable that I see:
i.   the need to keep eyes healthy–morality
ii. the need to serve one master – loyalty
iii. the need to not worry but have faith – dependence

In my several years in management, I have come to the conclusion that the character of the person that could be trusted with higher responsibility must include all these three parts.

A staffer whose eye is corrupt to the assets of and people within the company usually does not last until his/her corruptness is discovered and is let go. A single eyed person knows and is most often focused on where s/he is going versus a multi-directional, shifty, chameleon-like seeing-eye.

So also is the fact that when a staff shows allegiance/loyalty to corporate goals and objectives on a consistent basis, it is sure evidence that s/he could be rewarded or at least is on the same path with management and therefore was promotable to leadership position. Conversely, a staff that is constantly at odds with what the organization stands for in preference for competition ought to be given the opportunity of being let go, to explore where his loyalty lies.

Similarly, I have found out that the level of comportment or rather the temperament of a staff could also easily tell whether or not with added responsibility s/he would stay focused. A staff that worries stiff about every little thing and is constantly anxious about what s/he cannot get is telling me that s/he could not handle big issues and therefore might not last. So is the staff whose dependence extends only within his/her periphery as opposed to the one that might be disposed to asking for help beyond his/her limits.

The issue of faith and dependence on God of course is a biggie to me–in staying focused, if that faith includes prayers.

When a staff is entangled in immorality, disloyalty and ego-istic, self-centeredness, that staff could not be trusted because s/he has missed been focused on corporate goals and objectives and therefore cannot sell as material for leadership.

The second parable is also by Jesus and tells more of chokers that prevents focus. It is the Parable of the Sower. Hear how Jesus puts it:

""Then he told them many things in parables, saying: "A farmer went out to sow his seed…

and the seed fell among thorns, which grew up
and choked the plants. The seed falling among
the thorns refers to someone who hears the word,
but the worries of this life and the deceitfulness of
wealth choke the word, making it unfruitful.""–
Matthew 13:3, 7 & 22 [NIV]

It is not mere coincidence that Jesus here again highlights
the matter of worry and anxiety. You probably realize already
that besides being an entanglement, worry is also a choker. It
stifles good life and peace too, out of the most well-meaning.

But the real choker that I am ever so mindful of and run
away from is the deceitfulness of wealth or riches.

Before I proceed too far in this particular area, let me
quickly make a disclaimer:

I AM NOT IN ANY WAY OPPOSED TO BEING WEALTHY
– if acquired "right" and if it does not blind from reality
and fairness.

Having said that, it is honest to state that deceitfulness
of riches is not only a life choker, it blurs vision as well. It's
absolute deviation measure can best be outlier. It brings into
bondage and hardens the heart against anything called fairness. It deludes, corrupts and destroys. It is self-deception.

Jesus was teaching a lesson on deceitfulness of riches in
Luke 12:13-21. He noted that greed and dependence on abundance of wealth are both components of foolishness. The story
in this particular instance had to do with someone that the
Bible paradoxically referred to as "rich fool." In essence, his
riches made him develop myopic vision. To this rich man,
everything was about money: dollars and cents. Tear down
one small warehouse and build bigger... then become at ease
to drink, eat and be merry. It was all about "I", "me" and
"myself." He got choked by his great possession. He lost focus
for others and certainly also lost focus on God. He needlessly
passed on as a fool; losing his soul and all his boastful possession. Here was a bad consequence for losing focus on what
was important and necessary.

*When a staff is entangled in immorality, disloyalty and egoistic,
self-centeredness, that staff could not be trusted because
s/he has missed been focused on corporate goals and objectives
and therefore cannot sell as material for leadership.*

The story of the young ruler given by Jesus in Matthew 19:16-24 is a good warning against deceitfulness of riches. This was a man that knew everything that was needful about religion from his youth but was deluded about his "great possession." Following the Lord was to him an excess he could not afford. He lost his soul.

How about loving the world with the lust of the flesh and of the eyes and the pride of life with consequence of damning our souls?–I John 2:15-17

How about the admonition to not get overcome by the deceitful entanglement of the world? – II Peter 2:20

How about the exhortation to stay focused and not allow the faith that was once delivered to us slip? – Hebrews 2:1-2

But above all, Christians will do well to take the divine counsel to stay focused in Galatians 5:1 seriously so as to avoid devastating consequences:

> "Stand fast therefore in the liberty wherewith Christ has made you free. Don't be entangled again with the yoke of bondage." [KJV]

If society expects higher character standards from aspiring politicians, it will be simply foolhardy for Christians aspiring into leadership positions to possess less.

NITTY-GRITTY

Personally, I have found writing things down most helpful in staying focused. What with today's busy schedules that present themselves as all-important?

I do the yearly goals mostly at the turn of the year and break these down to monthly, weekly and daily schedules. I keep them few and manageable.

I create personal, family, Church and business goals and attempt to prioritize these by timing, importance and relevance. You must have heard of and possibly practiced the English terminology of "divide and rule" – i.e. reducing important matters into bite sizes. What a great idea.

Along with the annual goals and in order to stay steadfast in my commitment, I develop a "catch-phrase" for the year that is in line with my set goals. 2013 for example was my Year of Divine Favor; 2014 – my Year of Abundance and 2015 – my Year to ADVANCE. I remind myself of these catch-phrases in my prayers, my writings and speeches.

I do not tuck these away in some closet. I place them where I can keep an eye on them and pray over them: in my handy carry-about journal, on my weekly/daily to-do-lists and on the wall, often near enough to my office desk. I review them monthly to see if I was on track and to realign my timing and efforts – if I was off course.

Review also includes two little but important measures:

i.   to ensure that what I set out to do is/are actually what I needed – in the face of look-alikes. It had turned out few times, just few months down the road that what I thought I earlier set out to do and committed to had element of bias or unreality to it. With the passage of time, I probably have gotten wiser and could afford to strike such distraction off my list

ii. to understand the rationale for why I must commit myself to doing what I set out to do – just in case the level of importance and relevance have changed between the time I started and the time of my review.

What's more, I am not a big fan of television which I consider a major distraction. The television has a way of swaying your thoughts through the mind's eye. It is not that I dislike the artists/performers. Rather, I feel that spending too much time watching others will cut short the time I have in preparing for others to watch me. Plus the fact that I have been truly but ashamedly accused too many times that I sleep in front of television, just as it is true at the movie theater events – another indication that I consider these boring. So, I'll rather choose what keeps me awake: ensuring that I stay the course – regardless of attractions and distractions. Old school? Good school.

I am also not a party-goer/socialite. To few of my friends who would like for me to attend their events, this particular aspect doesn't go down well with them when they do not see me. Again, it is not that I like my friends any less, rather, it is that I would prefer to focus more on what will maintain our friendship – longer time: relevance to them and their cause. I realize that the reason they want me at their events is because they consider me relevant enough. And that should truly be a good test of who we really are to one another. If I seize to be relevant, you can be rest assured that they would staunchly prefer that I do not show up. So the game should therefore be to stay focused and relevant.

In this day and age, social media seems to be one overwhelming distraction. In the days of supposed "dummy" phones, you only access the internet through a desktop. You have a re-think before you mount the table, open the computer and punch in your user id and password. With today's "smart" phones, the distraction is heightened to red alert levels. You get your messages unsolicited – day and night. And unless you mute the smart phone ringer, you are severally distracted by incoming e-mails, instant messaging, Facebook, WhatsApp, Hangouts, twits, blogs and several other online chat forums.

For me, in order to stay focused, I try to limit my time for these, as much as possible, to evenings when I am more at ease.

Each person has to find the distraction triggers and try to plug and possibly pluck them.

I admit though that like most things, staying focused by plugging distractions is rather often easier said than done. Still, there can be no steady commitment to goals nor to achieving them without staying focused and this inextricably include some level of setting limits.

References:
[1] Jim Rohn's quote–http://www.brainyquote.com/quotes/quotes/j/jim-rohn120983.html
[2] Credit Suisse Report: http://economics.uwo.ca/people/davies_docs/credit-suisse-global-wealth-report-2014.pdf

PRINCIPLE SIX

Determine... to Be Purpose-Driven:

Choose what you do in the light of God's revealed plan and purpose about you   - **I Corinthians 7:17-24; Ephesians 4:1-16; I Corinthians 2:7-11**

*V*ery possibly one of the most read and impactful books of our time is the one written by Rick Warren[1] – *The Purpose Driven Life*. For several years, the Purpose Driven Life continued to make the headlines and remained a best-seller until it sold over 30 million copies.

Coming from a man that has gone through much of life's trials and deeply much of what God intends for mankind through faith and dependence on Jesus Christ, Rick Warren has been acclaimed by top hierarchy and governments as one of America's top leaders in the matter of being purpose-driven.

Interestingly enough, the animals and all created things, as part of God's designed ecosystem, know and function within the purpose for which they are created.

The trees: the olive, the fig, the vine, the cedar–all know why they are created [See–Judges 9:8-15]. The bramble, being an exception would prefer rather for mankind to metaphorically put their trust in a "shadow" of deception and tyranny that destroys.

And as if by constant rebuke, the Word of God also continues to caution us:

> "For the LORD has spoken: 'I reared children and brought them up, but they have rebelled against me. The ox knows its master, the donkey its owner's manger, but Israel does not know, my people do not understand.'" – Isaiah 1:2-3 [NIV]

> "Remember this, keep it in mind, take it to heart, you rebels. Remember the former things, those of long ago; I am God, and there is no other; I am God, and there is none like me. I make known the end from the beginning, from ancient times, what is still to come. I say, 'My purpose will stand, and I will do all that I please.' From the east I summon a bird of prey; from a far-off land, a man to fulfill my purpose. What I have said, that I will bring about; what I have planned, that I will do – Isaiah 46:8-11 [NIV]

YOUR LIFE ON PURPOSE

WHY AM I HERE?

Why do I exist? What purpose am I to serve?

It sure sounds like the unanswered question on the lips of many millions – possibly billions living today, and very likely on yours as well.

There are controversies among the learned and unlearned, the rich and the poor, the smart and the not-so-smart on the subject, mainly because of the notions passed down many generations as traditions. Christians of different denominations even differ on the reason for their existence.

What's more, I am confronted by well-meaning Christians who find themselves constantly struggling with the reason for existence, asking what in my opinion it could be. Many times, after listening to their stories, I am honest enough to tell them that I do not know. However, even when I think that I have a faint idea, I have all of the times referred them to the One who knows succinctly.

It will therefore not be fair to attempt by any stretch of imagination in this short space, to offer an in-depth study of why, as I believe, each one of us is here on earth. There are a lot of good Christian books written on the subject which are available in libraries and stores worldwide. See my suggested resources at the end of this chapter.[2]

At some of my speaking engagements, I have had the opportunity of defining who I am. This is what I often tell my audience, which by the way, is a coinage from what I heard my esteemed mentor said many years ago:

I was created in Heaven–for good works

I was assembled on Earth–for identity

I am now dispatched to my World–to be a blessing

I realized early enough in life that I am not just a number among God's creation. I am uniquely, fearfully and wonderfully made – for God's glory and to bless mankind.

Suffice it to say though, without necessarily sounding simplistic or making a seeming complex matter rather trivial, each of us has distinctive role we are expected to play in the grand scheme of God's creation.

There are things I am called to do which because I am endowed with the ability to do, find relatively easy and am passionate about. Someone else, trying to be me, will find the same things challenging and near unattainable. And of course, there are distinct abilities that the person who finds my passion challenging has which I might never be able to replicate – at least not as easily.

Collectively, we are created with distinct abilities for specific purposes, in order to make the whole creation "work" in synergy as desired by the Creator! Missing this purpose has resulted in the obvious "sweaty" chaos and self-destruction-universally: one man struggling to do someone else's mission and purpose – unknowingly and without the desire to know.

I was created in Heaven–for good works
I was assembled on Earth–for identity
I am now dispatched to my World–to be a blessing

Simply stated, we are created by Him and for His determined purpose, so we could truly experience the purpose for Jesus' coming: PEACE ON EARTH.

Imagine Jesus standing boldly right in front of intimidating Roman governor Pontius Pilate [AD 26-36] who was just about to hand down His crucifixion sentence and telling him to his face:

> "... To this end was I born, and for this cause
> came I into the world, that I should bear wit-
> ness unto the truth. Every one that is of the truth
> hears my voice."–John 18:37 [KJ2]

Each of the over seven billion humans living on Earth has been geographically and ethnically positioned and endowed with peculiar gifts [talents] to do roles only they alone could do with ease, for collective good. It behooves each one of us to discover what that purpose is and to passionately yet with determination pursue it.

The young psalmist turned King – David was aware of his reason for existence [Psalm 139:16] and sought the Lord on several issues for direction [I Samuel 23:9-12].

Prophet Jeremiah was aware of God's mandate on his life [Jeremiah 1:4-5].

Saul, turned Apostle Paul was a late starter but unmistakably heard the call of God while on a mission that he thought was for His defense [Galatians 1:13-17].

These all and countless others, just as Jesus said seemed to have unapologetically yet with submission chorused:

"Lo, [we] have come to do thy will O Lord…"– Hebrews 10:5-9 [KJV]

I have found out in my few short years that discovering our existence comes through "sincere" relationship with and love for God. To some this has come easy, while to others it has been with unease and yet to many – progressive, based on the degree of their yielding to God's will; what with the blaring pride and conceitedness. Humbling ourselves in prayer before this God has and will always get His attention and help in putting us on the path to knowing why we are here.

Perhaps with some level of comfort: seeking counsel from men and women of faith, of wisdom and integrity has helped many in getting to know who they are and what God may be calling them to do. I am in no doubt that this also takes swallowing our pride and summing up courage to ask mentors and peers counsel on the subject.

I am nonetheless fascinated by the familiar maintenance slogan on several products: "when in doubt, consult the manufacturer at the 1.800…."

Shouldn't it therefore stand to common reason that when there is a doubt as to man's reason for existence, he ought to get back to the Creator to discover through prayer, His intent and purpose for creating him? And when we are sensitive, sincere and obedient enough, we will always find out why.

And even though non-believers, evolutionists and atheists as creation of God ought to know, they may have made up their minds to live, not really caring, why they exist.

…discovering our existence comes through "sincere" relationship with and love for God.

137

I MAY NOT KNOW IT ALL, BUT...

It is possible that we may never know everything about our calling at once, but TRUSTING God at every step of the way will assure that we are on the right path.

Take the Apostle Paul for example, in his famous "focus" speech:

> "Not as though I had already attained, either were already perfect: but I follow after, if that I may apprehend that for which also I am apprehended of Christ Jesus. Brethren, I count not myself to have apprehended: but THIS ONE THING I DO, forgetting those things which are behind, and reaching forth unto those things which are before, I press toward the mark for the prize of the HIGH CALLING OF GOD IN CHRIST JESUS. Let us therefore, as many as be perfect, be thus minded: and if in any thing ye be otherwise minded, God shall reveal even this unto you. Nevertheless, whereto we have already attained, let us walk by the same rule, let us mind the same thing." Philippians 3:12-16 [NIV]

I hear Paul saying... "I have not fully attained," "I am not perfect," "There is a reason for my calling," "I'm just going to keep doing..." "I will leave myself open to God's continued and progressive revelation..."

Could these be the principles that fueled his ministry passion as he wrote half the Bible's New Testament: not knowing everything all at once?

"I have not fully attained," "I am not perfected,"
"There is a reason for my calling," "I'm just going to keep doing..."
"I will leave myself open to God's continued and progressive
revelation..."

DEFINE, DON'T CREATE

Few people on the planet have made so much contribution to modern business management as Peter Drucker.[3] His considerable focus on excellence in management is without any doubt commendable and cannot but be recognized by both for and non-profits. Not a few Churches and governments have benefited from his management consulting services.

However, with due respect to him and several of his devotees and setting prejudices aside, as much as I possibly can, I have a somewhat differing thought when it comes to his concept of "creating the future you desire."

I could argue that Peter Drucker was merely encouraging managers and aspiring leaders never to give up; rather, to have a forward-looking, forward-thinking mindset. But trying to create a future that would only be short-lived only to attempt another re-creation, to my mind, is synonymous with mere toil – under the curse.

While I am not a proponent of fatalism that demands total and unquestioning resignation to fate, simply because there is nothing man can do about his fate, I am nonetheless convinced of God's sovereignty in the affairs of mankind.

If mankind lives with the depressing weight of subservience to situations and circumstances, he has the privilege of going to God for a proper re-tooling.

Jabez in the Bible realized prominence when he defined his situation before God his Maker. He became more honorable than his brothers–by so doing [I Chronicles 4:9-10]

When David, the King of Israel saw himself in quagmire and desperate [Psalm 51:1-10], he did not struggle to create his future. Rather he asked God: "Create in me a clean heart, O God; and renew a right spirit within me."

139

When Saul turned Paul discovered his wretchedness, and in spite of the fact that he was notably learned [Acts 26:24], he refused to create a future for himself. Rather, he submitted to God as he cried: "O wretched man that I am! Who shall deliver me from the body of this death? I thank God through Jesus Christ our Lord." – Romans 7:15-25.

Adam tried the "creating his desired future" concept and it didn't appear to have worked. After sinning by deception, he and his wife realized that they were naked. And in their bid to create a "safe" future for themselves, went ahead, humorously I suppose, to create an apron "covering" out of leaves. Armed with excuses, as will always be the case with us all, when God returned in the cool of the day for a visit, they hid themselves and blamed their failure on someone else – the Serpent.

However, when at Gethsemane, the second Adam, laden with the cruel sins of the world, which He did not commit, faced with the dreadful cup of suffering and under the gruesome and agonizing pains of imminent death, He went back to His Father praying, with sweat like drops of blood:

> "...if you are willing, take this cup from me; yet
> not my will, but yours..."   – Luke 22:42 [NIV]

It is always in discovering and defining where we are at before the God of Creation – whether or not we needlessly sense being "a square peg in a round hole" that we get needed help. Not in struggling to create a future that leads to the land of unfulfilled destiny.

Adam tried the "creating his desired future" concept and it didn't appear to have worked. After sinning by deception, he and his wife realized that they were naked. And in their bid to create a "safe" future for themselves, went ahead, humorously I suppose, to create an apron "covering" out of leaves.

The idea that we will have to "create our desired future" is to my mind prideful and arrogates us to a status that we are not. It smacks of living the dung-beetle.

Defining our state of course must not be taken to mean that we become complainers or complacent without making efforts at doing "whatsoever our hands finds to do" with excellence. Neither does it advocate perfectionism. Rather it encourages returning to God, the Creator of the heavens and the earth, and letting Him have His way in our lives and to work that which is good in us. After all, the Bible is emphatic as to the fact that as Christians:

> "...we are God's handiwork, created in Christ Jesus to do good works, which God prepared in advance for us to do" – Ephesians 2:10 [NIV].

We are obviously God's work-in-progress, with continuous need for fixing, until we arrive at the yonder shore, to stand before the Judge of all and to give account of our works– Romans 14:12; Revelation 22:12

DRIVEN BY PURPOSE

Rick Warren's work "The Purpose Driven Life' lays out many compelling components. It's all about being purpose-driven and predicated on finding out the purpose for our existence.

However, most of mankind, from Adam till now has continued to be tempted and motivated into trying things out by our erroneous choices. We call it trial and error: our choice of spouses, career, hobbies, etc. The trial and error concept is characterized by repeated, varied attempts until we realize what we consider success – for that moment.

However, through trial and error, particularly in those important areas of our life, we have been severally burnt, yet like the dog returning to its vomit, have continued to repeat it, unmindful of the nauseating effect; the latest one resulting in worse consequence that the one before. We then wonder why we have had no distinctive success stories to tell or ever made enduring impact on our generation – even if modestly and at our little corner.

At such times, we are without a clear purpose and are at relative ease to change directions, jobs, relationships or churches at the drop of a hat.

Whereas the Lord Jesus Christ did nothing else, while He walked the streets of the Earth, other than to passionately honor God and be a blessing to humanity.

The Scriptures tell us in John 4:34 [NLT]...

> "My food," said Jesus, "is to do the will of him who sent me [my purpose] and to finish his work."

Again in Acts 10:38 [NLT]...

> "...God anointed Jesus of Nazareth with the Holy Spirit and power, and... went around doing good and healing all who were under the power of the devil, because God was with him."

Jesus was driven by the passion to honor God and to bless humanity.

Similarly when asked by one of the notable lawyers of Jesus' day what he was to do to get the full benefits of living, Jesus answered him in Luke 10:25-28...

> "What is written in the Law?" he replied. "How do you read it?" He [the lawyer] answered, " 'Love the Lord your God with all your heart and with all your soul and with all your strength and with all your mind'; and, 'Love your neighbor as yourself.'" "You have answered correctly," Jesus replied. "Do this and you will live." [NIV]

*At such times, we are without a clear purpose and
are at relative ease to change directions, jobs,
relationships or churches at the drop of a hat.*

We read of the olive tree, like other fruit trees and got a glimpse of what drives it, in his response when asked to do what it was not purposed to do:

"... why should I leave my fatness, with which
by me they honor God and man, and go to be
promoted over the trees?" – Judges 9:9 [AKJV]

That has always been the expectation of God for mankind: honoring God and blessing humanity.

That was also the pattern revealed to Apostle John, the writer of the Book of Revelation:

"Whenever the living creatures give glory, honor
and thanks to him who sits on the throne and who
lives for ever and ever, the twenty-four elders
fall down before him who sits on the throne and
worship him who lives for ever and ever. They
lay their crowns before the throne and say: "You
are worthy, our Lord and God, to receive glory
and honor and power, for you created all things,
and by your will they were created and have
their being." – Revelations 4:9-11 [NIV]

The realization of being created in Heaven–for good works; assembled on Earth – for identity and dispatched to my World, my generation–to be a blessing continues to drive me in keeping my purpose in focus.

I desire constantly to honor God through obedience and strive to take advantage of every opportunity to do good.

So the question that I ask you my reader is: what drives you?

Do you realize that you are God's masterpiece, His hand-iwork: created for good works and redeemed with a price? – Ephesians 2:10; I Corinthians 6:20

OPTIONS

One of the greatest challenges man has faced from creation continues to be that of making choices. From the Garden of Eden, Adam chose to believe the Serpent's lie. Every one from that time on had the choice where to pitch camp: with God or with the tempter – the devil.

That was one major error and an assault on the purpose for which man was created. It is the reason we are most often indecisive on life's major issues. Dare I suppose also that it is the common reason that our vision for God's purpose for our lives is blurred?

In today's culture of "leaving options open," we become trapped in failed relationships globally with the resultant frus-trations non-commitment brings.

It is commonplace to have parties to contractual terms pay more attention to "exit" clauses than the body benefit. Neither do I think that it is mere practice that the Wall Street has spe-cial attention paid to "options" and "hedging" as powerful investment strategies.

When we leave our options open, it becomes more diffi-cult to be determined or decisive. We then miss out on the meaning of patience, the relevance of commitment and the joys of living a purpose driven life. As replacement, we are handed the plaque of "easy-come-easy-go."

I have had the privilege of sitting in with my wife to counsel marriages and cannot but stop to wonder whether or not those once love-birds really meant the sacred vows that they took at their marriage ceremonies:

> "I ...., do take you .... as my wedded
> ...., to love and to hold, to comfort and honor,
> for better or for worse, for richer or poorer, in

sickness and in health, and forsaking all others…, as long as I live."

These once never-see-wrong, never-hear-evil couples, not very long after their vows soon began to get carried away by the luring attractions of options, easily discovering and comparing the shortcomings of the partner and becoming mean-spirited, nasty and seeing the partner as attempting to reach for each other's jugular. They made easy, yet wrong choices of non-committal, from the mindset of could-opt-out.

This non-committal paradigm shift seeps into most facets of life and has been responsible largely for society's moral decadence–globally. We say to ourselves to the point of assertion that we are "free moral agents." We assume that we have the right to choose and not be compelled.

I am convinced that the intent of our constitutional liberty was not to hang in a limbo of many choices and do wrong. It was rather, I will like to believe, to have the ability to express and follow through on what we consider as our purpose, for the best interest of our communities – just very similar to God's original intention of honoring God and serving man.

This non-committal paradigm shift seeps into most facets of life and has been responsible largely for society's moral decadence–globally.

How I wish we could have another Elijah standing not far away from where we all live and preaching to us as he did with the believers at Mount Carmel:

"How long will you waver between two opinions? If the LORD is God, follow him; but if Baal is God, follow him." – I Kings 18:21 [NIV]

Moses did not give Israel several options. He said to them:

145

> "This day I call the heavens and the earth as wit-
> nesses against you that I have set before you life
> and death, blessings and curses. Now choose life,
> so that you and your children may live and that
> you may love the LORD your God, listen to his
> voice, and hold fast to him. For the LORD is your
> life, and he will give you many years in the land
> he swore to give to your fathers, Abraham, Isaac
> and Jacob." – Deuteronomy 30:19-20 [NIV]

Joshua his successor followed suit. He did not give the leadership of his day open options. Bet if Joshua lived today, he will be amazed at the level of degeneration believers in God have sunk. Without any iota of a doubt, I feel convinced that he will not hold back in chiding us as he did with the leadership of Israel of his day:

> "...if serving the LORD seems undesirable to
> you, then choose for yourselves this day whom
> you will serve, whether the gods your ances-
> tors served ...in whose land you are living..." –
> Joshua 24:15 [NIV]

There were not too many options presented to the people of God those days until Francis Scott's famous "land of the free and home of the brave" began to take hold of our sensibilities and apply it as it were–in the wrong way.

*We have a God-ordained purpose and ought to choose
that purpose and nothing else.*

We have a God-ordained purpose and ought to choose that purpose and nothing else. We are called to honor God and serve humanity. But we have deliberately chosen to waver between opinions and to accept the permissive options of liberty, in order to serve the Baal of self.

146

Little wonder that we do not have many godly examples of successful leaders in our neighborhoods and little wonder then that aspiring leaders do not find good enough lessons on commitment and dedication to purpose?

CALLING

The topic of the Christian Calling has been confused severally with his Purpose.

Correctly understanding our purposes and calling will always help accelerate our fulfilling them.

I hope that you now know from my earlier explanation what forms the human Purpose, i.e. honoring [glorifying] God and blessing mankind.

Our purpose is fulfilled when all things that we do–in word or deed, are in the name of the Lord Jesus and for the glory of God the Father [Colossians 3:17].

Our calling does not get fulfilled if we fail to do what God desires of us.

For example if instead of being the dutiful, diligent, resourceful manager, we become slothful, sloppy and make little or no contribution to the advancement of the business purpose, we would not be answering our call.

It is possible to choose your calling: your career, your vocation or profession and be acclimated or trained to do it well, but if it is outside of God's purpose, you just might very well be living a life of disobedience with its concomitant consequences. You certainly must be running on someone else's lane and may very well be awaiting disqualification at the end of the race.

There are people who received specific calling for certain roles. There are specific mandates for specific assignments and specific needs of the hour.

Noah was to save **his household and establish posterity** for the world that would follow after the condemnation of the first sinful world – Hebrews 11:7

Abraham, the father of our faith was the first among many in that category. You probably remember how that when he

147

received the call to go out to **locate the city with foundations,** whose builder and maker is God Himself as the Promised Land, the Bible tells us: "... he went out..."–Hebrews 11:8

Moses was God's deliberate choice at His appointed time, to **lead the Jews out of the Egyptian enslavement** – Exodus chapters 2 through 12.

Jesus Christ came **to save God's creation** from a second destruction – Matthew 1:21

Paul was **"sent specifically to the Gentiles..."** – Romans 11:13

And on and on the list grows... Samson, David and the Kings of Israel, Esther, Nehemiah, Samuel and the prophets, the disciples of Jesus...

To some, it was establishing something new, to some others it was breaking down what had been wrongfully established, yet to several others, it was repairing what had been established with faulty foundations or unsettling structures.

Recognizing and staying at those calling has always been the critical issue of our society, nay of mankind–generally.

But one thing is very certain: There is a "gift," a "calling" given to each of us so we can help each other. Yours might be the ability to give wise counsel; mine might be of some knowledge, but the Spirit of God divides severally to all of God's children, so we all could help each other. – I Corinthians 12:1-31 [NLT]

And as if to make it more interesting, God foreknew each of us, predestined us and called us well in advance for these specific roles here on earth–Romans 8:29-32, 35-39 [NIV].

Interestingly enough, once we arrive here, he made provision for our justification, just incase someone or some situation were to attempt to distract us from those calling!

So we do not have to sweat the stuff – if we would constantly rely on Divine guidance. A specific one-time revelation might do for some–few. A progressive revelation might just very well be what numerous others need. But these all, with trust in and dependence on the Holy Spirit, coupled with continued obedience to His dictates can be rest assured to discover what God sent them to do.

All humans are created for God's glory and honor: one purpose. All humans are shaped delicately and uniquely suited for performance roles and expectations: different calling.

Our calling enables us to fulfill God's purpose for creating us.

A clearer understanding is the soccer game that I feel fairly familiar with: there is the owner, the coach and the players. Among the players, there is the goal-keeper, the mid-fielders, defenders, attackers, etc. These all form the soccer game team. The team could be part of a wider league but it is a body of its own, functioning uniquely. What's more, each member of the team needs to make required contribution to the collective effort in realizing the purpose of setting up the team – that of winning. Winning and remaining outstanding is their purpose. The roles which differ distinctly from one team member to the other form their calling.

When the purpose of the team is realized, the owner and the coach are honored and the players are rewarded for fulfilling their calling.

Borrowing King David's expression of his uniqueness:

> "For thou hast possessed my reins: thou hast covered me in my mother's womb. I will praise thee; for I am fearfully and wonderfully made: marvelous are thy works; and that my soul knoweth right well. My substance was not hid from thee, when I was made in secret, and curiously wrought in the lowest parts of the earth. Thine eyes did see my substance, yet being unperfect; and in thy book all my members were written, which in continuance were fashioned, when as yet there was none of them." – Psalm 139:13-16 [KJv]

We all, like David, are created and suited for performance roles only us can function at and be responsible for. A soccer player attacker, with all of his brilliance, exchanging places with the goal-keeper will ruin the collective efforts of the team. So will the team owner, with all of his influence, bullying his way as mid-fielder. Each member of the team knowing and functioning in his calling make the team work and by extension, team-work makes the dream work.

All of us generally have a purpose and reason for existence. Each of us has individual calling that enables us realize our purpose.

Jesus told us in John 4:34 [NLT]…

"My food," said Jesus, "is to do the will of him who sent me [my purpose] and to finish his work [my calling]."

Jesus also said in John 17:4 [NLT]…

"I have brought you glory on earth [my purpose] by finishing the work you gave me to do [my calling]."

In a nutshell:

"… we know that all things work together for good to them that love God, to them who are the called according to his purpose." – Romans 8:28 [KJV]

"[God] hath saved us, and called us with an holy calling, not according to our works, but according to his own purpose and grace, which was given us in Christ Jesus before the world began…" – II Timothy 1:9 [KJV]

"In Him we are called, being predestinated according to the purpose of him who works all things according to the counsel of his will." – Ephesians 1:11

Our calling enables us to fulfill God's purpose for creating us.

150

Ponder over these Scriptural exhortations:

"… as God hath distributed to every man, as the Lord hath called every one, so let him walk. And so ordain I in all churches. Is any man called being circumcised? let him not become uncircumcised. Is any called in uncircumcision? let him not be circumcised. Circumcision is nothing, and uncircumcision is nothing, but the keeping of the commandments of God. Let every man abide in the same calling wherein he was called. Art thou called being a servant? care not for it: but if thou mayest be made free, use it rather. For he that is called in the Lord, being a servant, is the Lord's freeman: likewise also he that is called, being free, is Christ's servant. Ye are bought with a price; be not ye the servants of men. Brethren, let every man, wherein he is called, therein abide with God–I Corinthians 7:17-24 [KJV]

I therefore, the prisoner of the Lord, beseech you that ye walk worthy of the vocation wherewith ye are called, with all lowliness and meekness, with longsuffering, forbearing one another in love; Endeavoring to keep the unity of the Spirit in the bond of peace. There is one body, and one Spirit, even as ye are called in one hope of your calling; One Lord, one faith, one baptism, one God and Father of all, who is above all, and through all, and in you all. But unto every one of us is given grace according to the measure of the gift of Christ. Wherefore he saith, when he ascended up on high, he led captivity captive, and gave gifts unto men. (Now that he ascended, what is it but that he also descended first into the lower parts of the earth? He that descended is the same also that ascended up far above all heavens, that he might fill all things.) And he gave some, apostles; and some, prophets; and some, evangelists; and some, pastors and teachers; For the perfecting of the saints, for the work of the ministry, for the edifying of the body of Christ: Till we all come in the unity of the faith, and of the knowledge of the Son of God, unto a perfect man, unto the measure of the stature of the fullness of Christ: That whence forth be no more children, tossed to and fro, and carried about with every wind of doctrine, by the sleight of men, and cunning craftiness, whereby they lie in wait to deceive; But speaking the truth in love, may grow up into him in all things, which is the head, even Christ: From whom the whole body fitly joined together and compacted by that which every joint supplieth, according to the effectual working in the measure of every part, maketh increase of the body unto the edifying of itself in love–Ephesians 4:1-16 [KJV]

RELEVANCE: THE TRUE TEST

Relevance: the true test of purpose and calling.

There are two sobering stories told in the gospels that every aspiring leader should read.

The first story appears in the gospel according to Matthew 21:18-20 [NIV]

"Early in the morning, as Jesus was on his way back to the city, he was hungry. Seeing a fig tree by the road, he went up to it but found nothing on it except leaves. Then he said to it, "May you never bear fruit again!" Immediately the tree withered. When the disciples saw this, they were amazed. "How did the fig tree wither so quickly?" they asked."

The other story appears in Luke's gospel 13:6-9 [NIV]

"Then he told this parable: "A man had a fig tree growing in his vineyard, and he went to look for fruit on it but did not find any. So he said to the man who took care of the vineyard, 'For three years now I've been coming to look for fruit on this fig tree and haven't found any. Cut it down! Why should it use up the soil?' " 'Sir,' the man replied, 'leave it alone for one more year, and I'll dig around it and fertilize it. If it bears fruit next year, fine! If not, then cut it down.' """

In both stories, there were expectations and there were consequences for failure to meet those expectations.

I consider that the same question could be apologetically asked in both instances: Of what relevance is a tree that has the potential of bearing fruits as many times as two or three seasonally, yet has nothing?

The trees, like humans without relevance, have enough of pretence, falsehood and deception quite alright except that they have little or no fruitfulness to show for their existence. Whereas, anyone with the right relationship to the True Vine will always "bear much fruit" of relevance – John 15:5-8

As I grew through the ranks and as a Christian committed to God's purpose and calling for my life, I am constantly reminded that I am His handiwork, created in Christ Jesus to do good works [Ephesians 2:10]. What He wants for me and from me, I determined upfront to be and do. In being and doing so, I have discovered relevance, joy and satisfaction.

I hear the Lord Jesus saying to me:

"You are the salt of the earth." – Matthew 5:13

"You are the light of the world. A town built on a hill cannot be hidden." – Matthew 5:14

"[You] ...are ambassador for Christ." – II Corinthians 5:20

But perhaps what I hear most loudly of these enviable positions are the cautions not to lose my essence, my relevance:

> "...if the salt loses its saltiness, how can it be
> made salty again? It is no longer good for any-
> thing, except to be thrown out and trampled
> underfoot." – Matthew 5:13

"If you put the light under the bushel, it will go out" –
Matthew 5:14

> "You could not be a believer for so long and still
> depend on milk; you are immature and a babe..."
> – Hebrews 5:12-13 [rendition mine]

It certainly cannot be enough to profess faith in the Lord
Jesus Christ. I have to manifest the relevance of my faith by
"good works." – James 2:14-26

What good is it, my brothers and sisters, if someone claims
to have faith but has no deeds? Can such faith save them?
Suppose a brother or a sister is without clothes and daily food.
If one of you says to them, "Go in peace; keep warm and well
fed," but does nothing about their physical needs, what good
is it? In the same way, faith by itself, if it is not accompanied by
action, is dead. But someone will say, "You have faith; I have
deeds." Show me your faith without deeds, and I will show
you my faith by my deeds. You believe that there is one God.
Good! Even the demons believe that–and shudder.

You foolish person, do you want evidence that faith without
deeds is useless? Was not our father Abraham considered
righteous for what he did when he offered his son Isaac on
the altar? You see that his faith and his actions were working
together, and his faith was made complete by what he did.
And the scripture was fulfilled that says, "Abraham believed
God, and it was credited to him as righteousness," and he
was called God's friend. You see that a person is considered
righteous by what they do and not by faith alone. In the same

way, was not even Rahab the prostitute considered righteous for what she did when she gave lodging to the spies and sent them off in a different direction? As the body without the spirit is dead, so faith without deeds is dead.

If our Master, the Author and Finisher of our faith left us example of relevance, it behooves us–His followers to be relevant to the needs of situations, circumstances within our community and on our watch.

It certainly cannot be enough to profess faith in the Lord Jesus Christ. I have to manifest the relevance of my faith by "good works."

"The PURPOSE of life is a life of PURPOSE."

Robert Byrne

References:
[1]**Pastor Rick Warren**: author of New York Times bestselling book – The Purpose Driven Life is the founder and Lead Pastor of Saddleback Church, Lake Forest, California. His Church is acclaimed to be America's 8th largest Church. http://en.wikipedia.org/wiki/Rick_Warren
[2]**Recommended Resources**: Chosen But Free, revised edition: A Balanced View of God's Sovereignty and Free Will by Norm Geisler;
The Potter's Freedom: A Defense of the Reformation and a Rebuttal of Norman Geisler's Chosen But Free by James R. White;
Created For Significance, [CDs] by Ravi Zacharias;
God in the Mirror: Discovering Who You Were Created to Be by Miles McPherson and
Why Are We Created? Increasing Our Understanding of Humanity's Purpose on Earth by
John M. Templeton & Rebekah A. Dunlap
[3]**Peter Drucker**: http://www.thefamouspeople.com/profiles/peter-drucker-132.php

PRINCIPLE SEVEN

Determine... to Be Closer To God than ever before:

...in Prayers, in Study of the Word, in Fasting, in Fellowship, in sharing your faith and experience, in obedience–James 4:8[a]; Psalm 37:4-5. Also Matthew 4:19-22

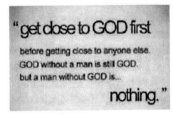

"get close to GOD first before getting close to anyone else. GOD without a man is still GOD. but a man without GOD is...

nothing."

*A*s a kid, I sang the song: "Jesus on the inside, working on the outside; Oh what a change in my life..." several times over and over again till friends, family and neighbors alike would hilariously ask which department of my body Jesus was working on at any time that I passed by. Then it was like a joke. Much later, it became an affirmation of my desire. That was when it made the difference between mere profession and heart belief; a time that I could attest to the true effects of salvation. It soon translated into my yearning to be a true

Christian with Jesus truly living on the inside and the passion to be drawn closer to God ever than before.

I also remember how we would often sing the song: "Take the whole world and give me Jesus" till the intent of the song was lost. We would sing it and stylishly yet defiantly, not wanting to have anything to do with the world. Those were the days when the television was regarded as the devil's box and anything fanciful, the glamour of and cuddling with the world – spoken against in I John 2:15-17.

We tried to live holy quite alright, except that it did not seem to draw us any closer to God as much as it flung us further away from humans. We certainly perfected the outward cleansing so much that the scribes, Pharisees and hypocrites of Matthew 23 would feel jealous of our copy-cat'ism. So at the end of the day, much as we seemed enthusiastic of heaven, we were lethargic and earthly inadequate. We profess religion quite alright, except that our piety has little or no enduring effect on our daily living.

It was all about talking the talk and not walking the walk.

> "The Lord says: "These people come near to me with their mouth and honor me with their lips, but their hearts are far from me. Their worship of me is based on merely human rules they have been taught. Therefore once more I will astound these people with wonder upon wonder; the wisdom of the wise will perish, the intelligence of the intelligent will vanish." Woe to those who go to great depths to hide their plans from the LORD, who do their work in darkness and think, "Who sees us? Who will know?" You turn things upside down, as if the potter were thought to be like the clay! Shall what is formed say to the one who formed it, "You did not make me"? Can the pot say to the potter, "You know nothing"?" – Isaiah 29:13-16 [NIV]

157

To make a determined difference, it is a no brainer that we first have a genuine relationship with God that influences us positively in becoming relevant for service to mankind. But drawing closer to God without corresponding relevance for service to mankind will, for all intents and purposes, be a useless proposition.

As Hebrews 4:16 tells us, it is in drawing closer to God that we discover the emptiness and inadequacies of mankind in order to find grace to fulfill our calling to help them in times of need.

...drawing closer to God without corresponding relevance for service to mankind will, for all intents and purposes, be a useless proposition.

WHAT A RARE PRIVILEGE!

The lengthy and most often arduous process of visiting and receiving eminent individuals could discourage the faint at heart. It is not uncommon to have a wide array of paraphernalia when meeting with dignitaries. But standing before monarchs deemed as deities could be a totally different experience.

Esther the Queen had a rare privilege. The background to her enduring prominence had been that of a masked threat by a palace high chief. The Jews were faced with decimation that was approved by the King of the land. Being a Jew herself and hearing of the plot, it was obvious that Esther was pre-ordained of the God of Heaven to foil it and to save the Jewish posterity. But it took more than just being the Queen. She and her people fasted and she put her life on the line as she did the impossible: presenting herself before the King–unscheduled. That was an offence punishable by death unless the King held out the golden scepter. Esther's life was spared as the King held out the golden scepter; her request for a royal dinner was granted and further down the road shortly after, the decree of death over the Jewish race was annulled. Talk of the power of privilege, nay, rare privilege!

Apostle Paul, many years later was describing the rare privilege of coming before the Lord of lords and the King over all earthly kings when he said:

> "…I reckon all things as pure loss because of the priceless privilege of knowing Christ Jesus my Lord…" – Philippians 3:8 [WEY]

But perhaps most striking is his narrative of the privilege in the Epistle to the Hebrews:

> "Therefore, brothers and sisters, since we have confidence to enter the Most Holy Place by the blood of Jesus, by a new and living way opened for us through the curtain, that is, his body, and since we have a great priest over the house of God, **let us draw near to God** with a sincere heart and with the full assurance that faith brings, having our hearts sprinkled to cleanse us from a guilty conscience and having our bodies washed with pure water. Let us hold unswervingly to the hope we profess, for he who promised is faithful." – Hebrews 10:19-23 [NIV]

Imagine the believer's very rare privilege of drawing near the Great and Almighty God, afforded–without his/her effort or righteousness but by the shed blood of Jesus.

There are no protocols to be observed other than coming in faith and realizing that He is a Spirit that must be worshipped as such. What a divine pleasure and favor – John 4:24

After all…

> "You have not come to a mountain that can be touched and that is burning with fire; to darkness, gloom and storm; to a trumpet blast or to such a voice speaking words that those who heard it begged that no further word be spoken

to them, because they could not bear what was commanded: "If even an animal touches the mountain, it must be stoned to death." The sight was so terrifying that Moses said, "I am trembling with fear." But you have come to Mount Zion, to the city of the living God, the heavenly Jerusalem. You have come to thousands upon thousands of angels in joyful assembly, to the church of the firstborn, whose names are written in heaven. You have come to God, the Judge of all, to the spirits of the righteous made perfect, to Jesus the mediator of a new covenant, and to the sprinkled blood that speaks a better word than the blood of Abel."–Hebrews 12:18-24 [NIV]

PRAYING...

Very possibly one aspect of the Christian life that is most often made light of is prayer. Not many believers take advantage of it's potency and certainly fewer experience the peace that comes through it.

It is easy to feel like not wanting to bother God with our needs and instead, feel presumptuous, thinking that we could handle life's challenges ourselves.

Prayerlessness weakens the Christian and when allowed over extended period of time, strips him of true spirituality, leaves him vulnerable to worldliness. When we are prayerless, we have nothing to look up to than ourselves and the world around us. We are drawn to the rat-race and the attendant vagaries that include disappointment, discouragement and ultimately depression.

It is in the secret place of prayer and of seeking God's face that we take cue from His thoughts and receive boldness, positive promptings and enduring encouragement.

It is where we begin our journey to making the determined difference.

160

The story of the Rich Fool told in Luke 12:16-21 is a good lesson on the need to draw closer to God, just so we are not carried away by conceit but rather to have Him as our dependency.

Whereas, the tendency is often to be self-centered and self-pleasing in life's matters, God would rather that we seek Him, acknowledge Him and depend on Him.

And in the Psalmist's exhortation, we need to delight ourselves in the Lord, love Him with all our heart, soul and strength and commit our ways to God, so He could give us the desires of our hearts – Psalm 37, Luke 10:27.

> *...one aspect of the Christian life that is most often made light of is prayer.*

Trusting the Lord with our affairs in prayer produces inward humility, draws us closer to God and keeps our heart out of trouble [James 4:7-10; John 14:1]. It actualizes the faith to "ask", "seek" and "knock."

It is primarily in prayer of commitment and the study of the Word that we feel the sense to draw closer to God. That is when we have our heart sprinkled with clean water of the Word–from evil conscience and it is also when we receive assurance of answered prayers – by faith [Hebrews 10:19-22].

Dependence on God gets easier through prayers – even if it is only to thank Him for what we have. After all, He created and owns all things in the first place.

When, like the Laodicean Church in Revelations 3 we think that we are all set, prideful and having need of nothing, it could very well be that we fail to realize how wretched, pitiful, poor, blind and naked we are – v.17. At such times and in such situations, it will be easy to get "spewed out" of God's mouth instead of being drawn closer to Him. Rather, those should be the times and situations when we need to be reminded to draw closer to God.

I confess that I didn't learn the lesson easily myself. At those times when I had everything covered – financially, I have been tempted to suppose that I was in charge. It just turned out that I was going farther away from reality and in essence, from God. Like the rich guy in Luke 12, I was blinded by the fact that since God had blessed me enough to care for my needs, there was little need to sound pious by ascribing it to God or to even bother bringing Him into the equation. I did it all and own them all – or so I supposed, until little by little, the fluff on my cushions were replaced by the harsh realities of settling discomfort. Then, I began to realize and acknowledge that God was the One that gave me the power in the first place, to get wealth [– Deuteronomy 8:18] and so learnt to retreat my steps in the direction of God: closeness.

It could not have been for the sake of filling the pages of the Bible that Apostle Paul included the exhortation:

> "Be careful for nothing; but in every thing by prayer and supplication with thanksgiving let your requests be made known unto God. And the peace of God, which passes all understanding, shall keep your hearts and minds through Christ Jesus." – Philippians 4:6-7 [KJV]

I like the fact that the exhortation was not to pray about few, limited concerns and worry about the rest. It was rather to approach God in prayer about everything! It is impliedly an exhortation to develop the nature, the habit of drawing close to God!

At those times when I had everything covered – financially,
I have been tempted to suppose that I was in charge.
It just turned out that I was going farther away from
reality and in essence, from God.

I also realized that God draws closer to us and is pleased when we ask Him "everything," everyday, from the littlest to the biggest enterprise. He wants them all brought to Him in PRAYER, supplication and with thanksgiving – unceasingly

[Philippians 4:6-7, I Thessalonians 5:17]. He is interested and wants us free from anxiety and the worldly cares.

A recent story credited to the popular Evangelist Reinhard Bonnke conveys the lesson on intimacy and trust that could only be developed through drawing close to Jesus. In the story, a Christian man allowed Jesus Christ into some space in his house but not all. He treated Jesus as a welcome guest but not Lord over all. When the devil came knocking, those spaces that he did not give to Jesus became vulnerable as the devil was wont to lay claim. The man soon realized that as he submissively gave Jesus access to all the spaces in his house did He really assume responsibility over "everything" and control over the intruding devil. What an impactful admonition to constantly draw close to God and letting Him be in charge of everything pertaining to us!

In making the determined difference, it becomes imperative that we know God and that we make efforts to draw closer to Him daily–James 4:8.

Could the prayer go without the study of the Word? Certainly not for long. Prayer without the study of the Word of God becomes a monologue: just speaking to God and not waiting to hear from Him. Many times God would speak to us through the still, small, inner voice. Most times, He already has spoken in His written Word which we could discover and learn wisdom from, on daily living.

An excellent way of drawing close to and relating with God is to engage in a two-way dialogue with Him, where we study His Word, sometimes on specific issues and use the lessons learned as prayer points.

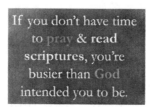

If you don't have time to pray & read scriptures, you're busier than God intended you to be.

BECAUSE OF HIS GREATNESS

I am humbled by Prophet Isaiah's declaration, affirming the greatness of God – under inspiration. Hear him:

> "Look up into the heavens. Who created all the stars? He brings them out like an army, one after another, calling each by its name. Because of His great power and incomparable strength, not a single one is missing." – Isaiah 40:26 [NLT]

> "As the heavens are higher than the earth, so are my ways higher than your ways and my thoughts than your thoughts." – Isaiah 55:9 [NIV]

Isn't it true that whatever is above us as humans and dwellers on the earth is beneath God that dwells high in the heavens? Yet in many instances when we're overwhelmed, we lose sight of this fact. We look for solutions from people and places where there are little, temporal or no help. And when those sources fail to produce desired results, we become agitated, irritated and offended. Worse still, when such sources include "close" friends or family members, it is not difficult to feel betrayed if they fail to meet our expectations. Whereas, if we had looked up to God at such difficult times, we would have sensed inner peace and comfort, realizing that God was in control – whether or not the help came from expected source.

Men and women of the Bible that did great exploits were always in communion with God. They drew close to God until like Moses, His glory began to radiate over them–Exodus 34:28

...whatever is above us as humans and dwellers on the earth is beneath God that dwells high in the heavens

Bible faith-worthies like Abel, Enoch, Noah, Abraham, Sarah, Isaac, Jacob, Joseph, Moses, Esther, Deborah, Rahab, Gideon, Samson, David and their likes drew closer to God in their relationship and commitment. By their closeness to and fervent faith Him, they changed their world – even in the face of tortures, cruel mocking, scourging and imprisonments. He in return strengthened their faith, their resolve and enabled them to accomplish what were thought humanly impossible including subduing kingdoms, stopping the mouths of lions, quenching the violence of fire, escaping the edge of the sword, valiantly driving back enemy armies...

They were men and women of prayer. They may not have been politicians, but they were the notable leaders of their days.

Apostle Paul represented it so well: relationship with Jesus Christ reflects on the dealings with people around us. Hear how his affection for Jesus influenced his wishes for the Philippians:

> "God can testify how I long for all of you with the affection of Christ Jesus. And this is my prayer: that your love may abound more and more in knowledge and depth of insight, so that you may be able to discern what is best and may be pure and blameless for the day of Christ, filled with the fruit of righteousness that comes through Jesus Christ—to the glory and praise of God." – Philippians 1:8-11 [NIV]

What is prayer any way? Isn't it talking with the God that you acknowledge can work things out for you because of His abilities? Communicating with the God that you have relationship with, trusting that as a true Friend, He will be there for you when you need Him?

In the days of Jesus Christ, there was a story told in Matthew 9:27-31, of two physically blind men who were spiritually sighted.

These guys followed Jesus wherever He went imploring His mercies. His question to them was poignant:

> "Do you believe that I am able to open your eyes?"

Just shortly before, they probably have heard of the healing of the leprous man, of the recovery of the army captain's sick servant, of the deliverance of Peter's mother-in-law from fever and of the many that were set loosed from the shackles of demonic power. And as if these were not enough, they were probably also told of how when a great storm bothered the disciples at sea, He rebuked and stilled it.

They reason among themselves: "a Man that can do these, what can He not do?"

They knew without any iota of the doubt of the greatness and ability of Jesus Christ to heal them.

They received their sight and went every where after that spreading the fame of Jesus.

Beyond just praying though, there was an instance where a man, realizing Jesus' greatness had knelt before Him to ask for the healing of his lunatic son. Earlier, Jesus' disciples had prayed over the boy without any respite. Once the boy was brought to Jesus, He rebuked the sickness out of him and he received deliverance instantly.

In their amazement, the disciples came to Jesus asking why the boy was not healed when they prayed. Jesus' response was quite revealing:

> "And Jesus said unto them, Because of your unbe-
> lief: for verily I say unto you, If ye have faith as
> a grain of mustard seed, ye shall say unto this
> mountain, Remove hence to yonder place; and
> it shall remove; and nothing shall be impossible
> unto you. Howbeit this kind goeth not out but
> by prayer and fasting." Matthew 17:20-21 [KJV]

It must be encouraging to know that simply praying without unbelief and with fasting can remove life's mountainous issues! Yet many professed Christians make light of prayer and worse still, many are scared to fast.

It cannot be a joking matter and certainly not a coincidence that several versions of the Bible took this all-important counsel out completely. That is what Satan wants! Don't pray and don't fast: so he could have the reins.

A proper perspective though is that fasting does not bribe God. It only humbles us, so we could deservedly acknowledge the almightiness of God

It cannot be a joking matter and certainly not a coincidence that several versions of the Bible took this all-important counsel out completely. That is what Satan wants! Don't pray and don't fast: so he could have the reins.

BUT WHY?

Be close to God? Why do I need to and where is He anyway?

There are times in all of our lives when we suppose that life deals us the wrong end. Those are the times when we feel beaten, betrayed and bleak. They are the times we feel down, discouraged, disillusioned and distressed. We probably have failed, faltered or even fallen. We then feel left, lost, lonely and longing for home. Things just don't seem to be working quite as we expect them, friends seem to have abandoned us, trust turned distrust, feelings are frayed and we are at our lowest ebb. No one quite understands what's going on inside of us but us.

Those are the times when we need the intimacy of the Designer and Sustainer of life; the One whose nature and integrity assures Omniscient [all-knowing], Omnipotent [all-powerful] and Omnipresent [all-present].

And only through the knowledge of and closeness to this God could we set our eyes in faith "above" to receive needed encouragement and strength at such times from the All-knowing, All-powerful and Ever-present in order to continue when all else fails.

Only through having a healthy relationship with God and by the power of His Holy Spirit could we experience divine intervention, such as could not be orchestrated by human hands.

At such times, we can rest in the assurance that Someone higher than us and the challenging situation we are in fully understands. He knows our inward thoughts and experiences.

David was at such point a number of times. You could read his testimony of the almighty-ness of the God in whom he believed:

"You have searched me, LORD, and you know me. You know when I sit and when I rise; you perceive my thoughts from afar. You discern my going out and my lying down; you are familiar with all my ways. Before a word is on my tongue you, LORD, know it completely. You hem me in behind and before, and you lay your hand upon me. Such knowledge is too wonderful for me, too lofty for me to attain. Where can I go from your Spirit? Where can I flee from your presence? If I go up to the heavens, you are there; if I make my bed in the depths, you are there. If I rise on the wings of the dawn, if I settle on the far side of the sea, even there your hand will guide me, your right hand will hold me fast. If I say, "Surely the darkness will hide me and the light become night around me," even the darkness will not be dark to you; the night will shine like the day, for darkness is as light to you. For you created my inmost being; you knit me together in my mother's womb. I praise you because I am fearfully and wonderfully made; your works are wonderful, I know that full well. My frame was not hidden from you when I was made in the secret place, when I was woven together in the depths of the earth. Your eyes saw my unformed body; all the days ordained for me were written in your book before one of them came to be. How precious to me are your thoughts, God! How vast is the sum of them! Were I to count them, they would

outnumber the grains of sand–when I awake, I
am still with you."–Psalm 139:1-18 [NIV]

What's more, as if to assure believers of His Omniscience,
Omnipotence and Omnipresence, Jesus Christ reiterated
"the God who sees in the secret" three times in the Gospel of
Matthew chapter 6:1-34 as He laid down the foundations of
victorious living, at difficult times, in His Sermon on the Mount.

I dare say that because He created all things for His pleasure [Revelations 4:11], there is NOTHING that is beyond
the power of our God [Luke 1:37]. To Him therefore must all
people come [Psalm 65:2].

This God is our God for ever and ever. He will be our guide
and our sure help in times of need – even unto the very end
[Psalm 46:1-11; 48:14].

It used to be that God would manifest Himself on mountains [Exodus 24] and through situations and circumstances
that were manifestly convincing it was Him [Exodus 13:20-
22]. Children of Israel must of necessity cleanse themselves
before drawing near to God at such places or circumstances or
they would be dead. Along the wilderness journey, God would
dwell in a Tabernacle. He gave specific rules on how to come
before His presence. There was the Holy Place and beyond
it the Holy of Holies. No one could come unclean near the
Tabernacle not to talk of going into it or into the Holy of Holies.
Only the representatives of God or the priests were allowed in.
These were deemed clean by the reason of the Sacrifice. And
even though the Tabernacle was mobile it was nonetheless
functional. It was a sacred place and the "Tent of Meeting."
Any discovered uncleanness of God's people necessitated a
"stop and get right" quarantine [The Book of Leviticus].

Once they arrived at the Promised Land though, the mobile
unit became increasingly vulnerable as the Ark of God dwelt
in tents – even though structurally more permanent.

Thus David the King was motivated down the road to build
one of such magnificent Tabernacles as God's dwelling place

[I Chronicles 17:1] in which His people were to come both to worship and to ask petitions of Him [II Chronicles 6 & 7].

But as important as the Tabernacle was to Israel, it was to the Creator of the heaven and earth Himself that David turned when in trouble:

> "I lift up my eyes to the mountains–where does my help come from? My help comes from the LORD, the Maker of heaven and earth. He will not let your foot slip–he who watches over you will not slumber; indeed, he who watches over Israel will neither slumber nor sleep. The LORD watches over you; the LORD is your shade at your right hand; the sun will not harm you by day, nor the moon by night. The LORD will keep you from all harm–he will watch over your life; the LORD will watch over your coming and going both now and forevermore." [Psalm 121:1-8] [NIV]

Little wonder that Apostle Paul many years after, disabused the minds of the superstitious Athenian worshippers that it was not about the Tabernacle, but God Himself that mattered in their worship [Acts 17:22-31].

Again, Jesus acknowledged and Stephen as well, before the Sanhedrin of his day, that the true God dwells in heaven and He uses the earth as His footstool [Matthew 5:34-35; Acts 7:49]. He lives above: far above our limitations, weaknesses and failures; above principalities and powers; above spiritual wickedness in heavenly places!

Moses drew near to God as he sought His face when hard-pressed by sinning Israel. As he approached the intimidating enemies along the way to Canaan, Moses needed the assurance of God's presence. It was in the quietness of fellowship that he had the rare privilege of God showing him His glory [Exodus 33:12-23].

Prophet Elijah was threatened by Jezebel – Ahab's wife after he had successfully confronted and withstood the husband

King Ahab and his prophets of Baal at Mount Carmel. That was a feat unequalled before the time: symbolically rebuilding Israel's altar that had been polluted, the calling down of fire from heaven and the slaying of Jezebel's prophets of Baal [I Kings 18]. But it seemed unrealistic that the bold Prophet would chicken out by a feminine intimidation.

Again in that state, void of the "unsettling" great and strong winds that shook the mountains, void of the "distracting" earthquake and fire but in quietness, he drew closer to God than ever before. Surely, God met with him at Mount Horeb in a still small voice and encouraged him [I Kings 19] to continue fulfilling the purposes of God – in Hazael, Jehu and ultimately his successor, Elisha. Jezebel was later taken out – just as it was prophesied.

Apostle Paul's exhortation to drawing closer to God in time of challenges is worth noting:

"Watch out for those dogs, those evildoers, those mutilators of the flesh. For it is we who are the circumcision, we who serve God by his Spirit, who boast in Christ Jesus, and who put no confidence in the flesh–though I myself have reasons for such confidence. If someone else thinks they have reasons to put confidence in the flesh, I have more: circumcised on the eighth day, of the people of Israel, of the tribe of Benjamin, a Hebrew of Hebrews; in regard to the law, a Pharisee; as for zeal, persecuting the church; as for righteousness based on the law, faultless. But whatever were gains to me I now consider loss for the sake of Christ. What is more, I consider everything a loss because of the surpassing worth of knowing Christ Jesus my Lord, for whose sake I have lost all things. I consider them garbage that I may gain Christ and be found in him, not having a righteousness of my own that comes from the law, but that which is through faith in Christ–the righteousness that comes from God on the basis of faith. I want to know Christ–yes, to know the power of his resurrection and participation in his sufferings, becoming like him in his death, and so, somehow, attaining to the resurrection from the dead. Not that I have already obtained all this, or have already arrived at my goal, but I press on to take hold of that for which Christ Jesus took hold of me. Brothers and sisters, I do not consider myself yet to have taken hold of it. But one thing I do: Forgetting what is behind and straining toward what is ahead, I press on toward the goal to win the prize for which God has called me heavenward in Christ Jesus."

- Philippians 3:2-14 [NIV]

In sum total, it must be told that it is all about drawing closer to and not withdrawing from God when faced with life's challenges that gets us the victory and ultimately assures our determined difference.

EXPECTATIONS

It is in the desires of the heart, in the unseen motivation, that many well-meaning Christians are put to the test – whether or not they really want to please God and serve mankind or no. Whether we seek God's glory or vaunt man's conceitedness.

Solomon the wise puts it this way:

"Let someone else praise you, and not your own mouth; an outsider, and not your own lips. The crucible for silver and the furnace for gold, but people are tested by their praise."–Proverbs 27:2, 21 [NIV]

It might be a good test for everyone seeking leadership role to step back once in a while to check his/her motive as well as responses and reactions. The one with the right mind

172

and motive will be more than happy to please God even if and when men's accolade is wanting.

Motivation, from foolery to flattery, to deluded ambition, a man ought to examine his heart each time the opportunity knocks for service. In a system of instant reward and celebration, fewer and fewer well meaning aspiring leaders are able to avoid the trappings of self aggrandizement: fame, wealth and status.

Pleasing God becomes secondary. Rather, it gets easier to hop on the bandwagon of relative ease, asking: "what's in this for me?" instead of a fervent desire to honor God and to do what He called us to do in the situation–in the first place.

Baruch in the Bible book of Jeremiah [45:1-5] was a talented journalist. He had served as the scribe to the Prophet Jeremiah until perhaps as acquaintances began to flatter how so important he was, being the scribe to a popular prophet. From nowhere, he started to feel that he deserved more. He very possibly was gunning to become the Editor-In-Chief of the prophet's news magazine – a chance position he thought could give him greater prominence and earn him more money. In the midst of a nation going through turmoil and Jerusalem facing plundering, Baruch saw what he thought was an opportunity of a lifetime. But little did he know that the Lord God above was listening to his heart's readings. God's reaction was:

> "Are you seeking great things for yourself? Don't do it…!" Jeremiah 45:5 [NLT]

Yet another poignant story was told in the Book of Acts of the Apostles. The setting was the spreading of good news and healing of the sick in Samaria. The city was receiving an unusual Divine visitation in the hands of the Apostle Philip and others. What followed was the Holy Spirit's baptism ministered by Apostles Peter and John. Many were saved, healed and delivered. In the midst of all these was a man simply called Simon the Sorcerer. He was said to have also believed with several others as Apostle Philip preached the Word of

God. He submitted himself for water baptism and was present when Peter and John were ministering the baptism in the Holy Spirit. Offering them money, he asked… "Give me also this power, that on whomsoever I lay hands, he may receive the Holy Ghost…"

That was his undoing.

Apostle Peter looked straight into his eyeballs and told him –

> "Thy money perish with thee, because thou hast thought that the gift of God may be purchased with money. Thou hast neither part nor lot in this matter: for thy heart is not right in the sight of God."–Acts 8:20-21 [KJV]

Heart not right with God because of wrong motivation!

It might be a good test for everyone seeking leadership role to step back once in a while to check his/her motive as well as responses and reactions. The one with the right mind and motive will be more than happy to please God even if and when men's accolade is wanting.

Jesus admonishes how we should present ourselves when we discover that calling of our lives:

> "So likewise ye, when ye shall have done all those things which are commanded you, say, 'We are unprofitable servants: we have done that which was our duty to do.'"–Luke 17:10 [KJV]

> "…do good, and lend, hoping for nothing again; and your reward shall be great, and ye shall be the children of the Highest:" Luke 6:35 [KJV]

> "Jesus saith unto them, 'My meat is to do the will of him that sent me, and to finish his work.'" John 4:34 [KJV]

"For I came down from heaven, not to do mine own will, but the will of him that sent me." John 6:38 [KJV]

"Consequently, when Christ came into the world, he said, "Sacrifices and offerings you have not desired, but a body have you prepared for me; in burnt offerings and sin offerings you have taken no pleasure. Then I said, 'Behold, I have come to do your will, O God, as it is written of me in the scroll of the book.'" Hebrews 10:5-7 [ESV]

"And though I have no wish to glorify myself, God is going to glorify me. He is the true judge." John 8:50 [NLT]

Apostle Paul, as if echoing Jesus' counsel also reiterates…

For I say, through the grace given unto me, to every man that is among you, not to think of himself more highly than he ought to think; but to think soberly, according as God hath dealt to every man the measure of faith. Romans 12:3 [KJV]

It just happens most of the time that the people who do the things that count do not count the things that they do.

The lyrics of the song "I just want to be where You are" by the popular American singer-songwriter, Pastor Don Moen touches hearts whenever sung. The lyrics of that song include the following:

- I just want to be where You are, dwelling daily in Your presence
- I don't want to worship from afar, draw me near to where You are
- I want to be where You are, dwelling in Your presence
- Feasting at Your table, surrounded by Your glory
- In Your presence, that's where I always want to be
- I just want to be, I just want to be with You

NO WHERE ELSE

A young man was tired of parental controls and after high school graduation, decided it was time to get a clean break from the unending "this is our house and you cannot do this and that...." On a rather happy morning, or so the parents thought, he woke up, dressed in work clothes and a back-pack, took off, unbeknown to them that that was going to be the last for a long time, they would see their teenage son. He told dad and mom he heard that the construction company downtown was hiring and he was going to check it out, perhaps there was an opportunity there for him.

From the little savings he had working during prior summers, he bought a one-way plane ticket to the farthest city on the west coast. He had no friends, no family and no acquaintance. He landed in this beautiful city at night, hung around at the airport – as if he was catching a transfer flight, and armed with a game plan, set out early in the morning into the city-center. He went from one shop to the other, looking for "we're hiring" signs. He found few and stopped to fill the employment applications. He also visited the city's public library ever so often, going online to check for vacancies. He e-mailed his now fear-filled mom that he had finally decided to leave home and that they should not bother to look for him because he was tired of the home rules. He assured them that they would be contacted if he needed their help.

Heartbroken and disappointed, the parents e-mailed back wishing him the best of luck. They also asked his exact location which he refused to disclose.

Luckily enough, within a couple of weeks, he got his first job which did not last. Within the first eight months of arriving in the bubble, he had worked in three organizations.

It was not long after that he got attracted to the way of life in the big city and throwing caution to the winds, joined himself to gangs.

Long story short, a number of years after leaving home, and now an adult, he was incarcerated for an alleged crime he never committed. He was to languish in jail for a long time

– without parole. His parents were contacted quite alright except that it was not by him as he had promised earlier.

Feeling crushed and disappointed, they made the gruesome journey to visit their son in prison on the other side of the country, wondering as they went, what to make of it all and how it could have gotten so bad with someone they thought they were raising with good character.

Escaping? Yeap. This story sounds very much similar to the Bible stories of the prodigal son in Luke chapter 15 and the Prophet Jonah of Jonah chapter 1 except that those had some divine encounter that helped them to return.

David, the King of Israel and renowned Psalmist was wiser. Every time that he did something wrong, he knew where to go: closer to God, not farther from Him.

Once, David in an apparent feat of pride, perhaps of cowardice dear I say, called for a census of the nations of Israel and Judah, which displeased the Lord. The word of the Lord in judgment came to his seer – Prophet Gad. He called David the king and told him what God was saying:

> "'This is what the Lord says: I am giving you three options. Choose one of them for me to carry out against you.' " So Gad went to David and said to him, "Shall there come on you three years of famine in your land? Or three months of fleeing from your enemies while they pursue you? Or three days of plague in your land? Now then, think it over and decide how I should answer the one who sent me." David said to Gad...
>
> "I am in deep distress. Let us fall into the hands of the Lord, for his mercy is great; but do not let me fall into human hands."–II Samuel 24:12-14 [NIV]

Without necessarily being judgmental, I dare say that Prophet Eli did not appear so smart when confronted with similar circumstance. His words at God's displeasure over his sons' blasphemous and unrestrained sinful lifestyle were: "It is the Lord, let Him do what He likes." – I Samuel 3:18.

Little wonder then that David experientially knew what it meant to draw close to God:

> Where can I go from your Spirit? Where can I flee from your presence? If I go up to the heavens, you are there; if I make my bed in the depths, you are there. If I rise on the wings of the dawn, if I settle on the far side of the sea, even there your hand will guide me, your right hand will hold me fast. If I say, "Surely the darkness will hide me and the light become night around me," even the darkness will not be dark to you; the night will shine like the day, for darkness is as light to you. For you created my inmost being; you knit me together in my mother's womb. I praise you because I am fearfully and wonderfully made; your works are wonderful, I know that full well.–Psalm 139:7-14 [NIV]

Smart guy: when he sinned, displeasing God at doing census; when he committed adultery with Bathsheba and killed Uriah her husband, he knew that there was nowhere else to run, except to the Lord–in repentance.

Escaping? Yeap. This story sounds very much similar to the Bible stories of the prodigal son in Luke chapter 15 and the Prophet Jonah of Jonah chapter 1 except that those had some divine encounter that helped them to return.

What a contrast and a determined difference!

LOYALTY

There would be no closeness to God if there has been no loyalty to Him primarily. And because of loyalty to God, the fruit of the Spirit: love, joy, peace, forbearance, kindness, goodness, faithfulness, gentleness and self-control rubs off on the believer and influences work and co-workers.

It is loyalty that produces commitment and that makes the Christian distinctly and determinedly different among many his equal. It is what convinces employers that the worker could be trusted and as such given leadership role.

When we know what God calls us to do, it is easier to be loyal.

In my days as I worked up the corporate ladder, loyalty meant convincing the employer that you like the organization and the job and so stayed put for many years. Workforce retention does not seem to matter as much today as with "brute" productivity. Everything including humans becomes components of production process. It used to be that humans tended machines and so needed to be encouraged in order to perform temperately, now machines give humans error messages when they do it wrong. And that is good to the extent that it minimizes rejects and imperfections. But production without relationship cannot but be boring. Productivity without closeness to the management, which comes through mutual trust, cannot guarantee sustainable success. So in this fast-paced, rapidly changing work environment, I guess that the more organizations that the worker is able to hop-in and hop-out, the more attractive his resume and the greater his appeal to prospective employers. Loyalty takes the back burner. That was not so.

Knowing what God called you to do enables you to operate in and celebrate the niche – in good as well as in bad times. That is what closeness to God teaches: giving the time and commitment to causes that we believe in and the readiness to stick it through until the desired change comes. It drives excellence and encourages superior service. It produces job satisfaction. In turn, the worker is appreciated. That is what devotion

179

is about. Loyalty is colored and becomes opportunistic when it's just all about recognition and perks.

However, should we determine that our contribution in a particular location or situation has ended, it has never been wrong to move to the next.

Yet for the Christian, it has to be within the leading and dictates of the Holy Spirit.

Also for the Christian, sincere closeness to God helps build closeness and strong character-based relationships with others. These translate in true friendships built on loyalty to one another. It overlooks errors and does not thrive on stigmas.

The Bible admonition to Timothy which I find appropriate on loyalty was:

> "... keep your head in all situations, endure hardship, do the work of an evangelist, discharge all the duties of your ministry. For I am already being poured out like a drink offering, and the time for my departure is near. I have fought the good fight, I have finished the race, I have kept the faith. Now there is in store for me the crown of righteousness, which the Lord, the righteous Judge, will award to me on that day–and not only to me, but also to all who have longed for his appearing." II Timothy 4:5-8 [NIV]

Child of God, stay steady, stay loyal, endure, do what you are called to do; there is a reward.

PRINCIPLE EIGHT

Choose... to Be Mentored:

"...Just as a nursing mother cares for her children, so we cared for you. Because we loved you so much, we were delighted to share with you not only the gospel of God but our lives as well."
I Thessalonians 2:7-8 [NIV]

On assuming the substantive position as a manager while climbing the corporate ladder, I had a mentor that gave me a profound counsel that became the foundation of my success in leadership.

He told me from the very get-go that if I desired an enduring success, I needed to present a teachable mind at all times. He wasn't really today's version of the tongue-speaking charismatic believer-mentor, but his words then and now sounded and still sounds profound and compelling.

And by the way, effective mentors, especially Christian mentors do not necessarily have to have all the answers, but as resource and guide to their mentees, they stand with them through the process of ascertaining what is best among many options, in realizing their mentees' God-given mandate.

My mentor's counsel was the difference between and actually the contrast to vaunting my smartness and the pride of not wanting someone to tell me what to do with my life and whether or not I really desired to be successful – long-term.

He had traveled the path I was embarking and served as my guide. He was willing to partner with me in order to reach my goal and I gained his trust. He shared useful hints with me and warned me of dangers and common pitfalls along the path. He made that segment of my journey less burdensome, for which I am eternally grateful.

To be sure, I never really liked failure, so I made determined efforts not to fail, from when I started to get aware of my God-ordained purpose and calling. But my desire for success did not substitute for necessary encouragement from mentors.

An English poet back in the 18th century – John Gay was credited with what I have held so dear in mentoring. He said:

"Tell me and I forget. Show me and I remember.
Involve me and I understand."

Like every human, and perhaps now to excuse myself for those years of silliness, I was for a long time prideful and self-centered. But once my mentor hashed out his "stay humble" counsel, I knew that I needed to start sooner than later, bringing my body, heart and mind under some form of control and subject to mentoring.

"In the same way, you who are younger, submit yourselves to your elders. All of you, clothe yourselves with humility toward one another,

182

because, "God opposes the proud but shows favor to the humble." Humble yourselves, therefore, under God's mighty hand, that he may lift you up in due time." – I Peter 5:5-6 [NIV]

"Similarly, encourage the young men to be self-controlled. In everything set them an example by doing what is good. In your teaching show integrity, seriousness and soundness of speech that cannot be condemned, so that those who oppose you may be ashamed because they have nothing bad to say about us." – Titus 2:6-8 [NIV]

It is an understatement to say that the times we live in today demand, more than ever before, that we swallow our pride and sing Bill Withers' "We all need someone to lean on." We need someone in our lives who could tell us the hard and unpolished truth, so we could have at the very least, some semblance of sanity.

He was willing to partner with me in order to reach my goal and I gained his trust. He shared useful hints with me and warned me of dangers and common pitfalls along the path. He made that segment of my journey less burdensome, f or which I am eternally grateful.

Speaking of myself, I recollect how my breaking came – at least on one supposedly inconsequential occasion. I had a rather trivial on-the-job argument with someone older than me. I did not see his point of view nor buy it. And in my undiplomatic style told him he was wrong. Sure enough, he backed down but then told me publicly shortly after and without any sugar-coating how prideful I was. He asked me: "What's this your bravado about?"

Boy, did that bother me months unending? You bet. However, it was the first time I went on a reality-check of myself.

183

I was afraid for a while and reserved for some more time. It instilled in me however, the need to watch my words and actions and I still do till now. It taught me that no matter what I thought I knew. there usually are others who know better than me. But the effect longer-term produced my quest for someone who would mentor me and tell me whether or not I was doing it right.

That's when we all need a mentor: someone who would gently yet firmly counsel us without necessarily directing or condemning us – a parent figure.

And I sense that today's younger generation, whether believers or non-believers, far from wanting it their way, desires some guidance, even if cautiously, some gentle baton-passing from older generations, so they could learn the art and culture of enduring success through their connection. There is the yearning, whether or not recognized, for wanting to learn from the experiences of those who may have walked their paths.

All through the Bible history, successful men and women of faith received mentoring:

Moses was mentored by Jethro, his father-in-law. He then mentored Joshua and the seventy elders.

Eli mentored Samuel who mentored Saul and David.

David mentored Solomon.

Elijah mentored Elisha.

Naomi mentored Ruth, the great, great, great grand-mother of our Lord Jesus.

Daniel mentored Nebuchadnezzar.

Esther received mentoring from her uncle – Mordecai.

Gamaliel mentored Paul

Paul mentored Timothy.

Jesus had many followers, but only twelve received direct mentoring from Him. These turned their world inside out and upside down.

That's when we all need a mentor: someone who would gently

*yet firmly counsel us without necessarily directing
or condemning us – a parent figure.*

No matter how good classroom education may be, there is always a priceless place for more effective learning when we sit side-by-side with someone that has been there and done it.

If you want to be fulfilled, present a teachable spirit and be ready to be mentored by someone you could gain his trust.

WALKING THE TIGHT-ROPE

Many years ago, I knew of this Pastor who lived carelessly. He met the Lord while in the prison and because he was so wildly passionate in his profession of faith, he was set free on the grounds of faithfulness. He went to the Bible School and further showed commitment to the Lord. Soon after, he was out of the Seminary and led a Church as its Pastor, but was to be mesmerized by the alluring connection to a younger Christian of the opposite sex – in the Church, who accused him of rape.

When confronted, he denied it, claiming that he was being victimized. Shortly after, the Committee investigating the allegation brought him and the young lady together and again, right in the presence of the lady, the Pastor's wife went after her, thinking she was about to tarnish the husband's glowing image and ministry. It became a drama which did not last too long.

The young lady, pointing to certain parts of her own body quietly asked the wife: "If you think I was lying, would you rather that I describe your husband's body marks and peculiarities?" What a bomb that was. Ashamedly, that sealed the accusation.

This was the same Pastor that was continuously warned by one of his Church Elders, but who always thought that the Elder was witch-hunting.

In this Pastor's case though, he was living a rather difficult tight-rope. No body cared to check his area of weakness: his viewpoints, attitudes and habits, before coming to the Lord or perhaps he was tight-lipped about it until it took control of him. I believe that a mentoring relationship would have revealed his spiritual needs and be guided on how to prevent a relapse. He, in my opinion should have been ministered to first, before expecting him to minister to others. He may have been saved needless embarrassment.

Showing interest and craving spiritual milk may be good, it is necessary for mentees to grow beyond it into a state of solid food, into spiritual maturity – I Peter 2:2-3

After all, as Paul would say in Hebrews 5:13-14:

> "Anyone who lives on milk, being still an infant, is not acquainted with the teaching about righteousness. But solid food is for the mature, who by constant use have trained themselves to distinguish good from evil." [NIV]

Suffice to suggest that coming from feeding on milk one day and going to solids the next–without mentoring, may have inadvertently set people like this Pastor up to fail.

Jesus would not send His disciples out without first properly mentoring them. His style of mentoring was distinctly worth emulating:

> "Jesus knew that the Father had put all things under his power, and that he had come from God and was returning to God; so he got up from the meal, took off his outer clothing, and wrapped a towel around his waist. After that, he poured water into a basin and began to wash his disciples' feet, drying them with the towel that was wrapped around him. He came to Simon Peter, who said to him, "Lord, are you going to wash my feet?" Jesus replied, "You do not realize now what I am doing, but later you will understand." "No," said Peter, "you shall never wash my feet." Jesus answered, "Unless I wash you, you have

no part with me." "Then, Lord," Simon Peter replied, "not just my feet but my hands and my head as well!" Jesus answered, "Those who have had a bath need only to wash their feet; their whole body is clean. And you are clean, though not every one of you." For he knew who was going to betray him, and that was why he said not every one was clean. When he had finished washing their feet, he put on his clothes and returned to his place. "Do you understand what I have done for you?" he asked them. "You call me 'Teacher' and 'Lord,' and rightly so, for that is what I am. Now that I, your Lord and Teacher, have washed your feet, you also should wash one another's feet. I have set you an example that you should do as I have done for you. Very truly I tell you, no servant is greater than his master, nor is a messenger greater than the one who sent him. Now that you know these things, you will be blessed if you do them." – John 13:3-17 [NIV]

You will notice interestingly that Jesus' mentoring style here was void of shouting bout, yelling or stick wielding. It was simply a dialogue of guidance and subtle appeal to humility – just as they saw Him did.

In today's convoluted world of "do as I say, not as I do," it stands to reason and indeed important to have quality mentoring of aspiring leaders by experienced, sometimes older persons on learning how to make character-based, enduring impact on society – just as the disciples of Jesus learned from Him. That, to my mind is how we can make a determined difference.

This Pastor's case may sound more like an outlier, but I do not think so. There are countless others out in our communities, who though are thought to be infallible, live carelessly daily, not paying attention to their weaknesses or rather, idiosyncrasies.

They vaunt the fact that they have relationship with the Lord who could teach them all they needed to know. By implication, they make light of their need for mentoring. Any wonder why many aspiring leaders fail and fall ever so soon on their rise to stardom? They are half-baked of course, being so egocentric and having no one to bounce their thoughts, actions and ideas off on for guidance.

These, like our Pastor friend could benefit immeasurably from "wise" mentoring.

"Anyone who lives on milk, being still an infant, is not acquainted with the teaching about righteousness. But solid food is for the mature, who by constant use have trained themselves to distinguish good from evil." [NIV]

Mentoring
Makes a Difference

MODALITY

I figure that someone reading this book might be curious on how to receive mentoring and the frequency.

Because mentoring should really be a lifelong affair, I will submit that it may be adapted to momentary needs, with the option of flexible, on-going appraisal by those mentoring.

Some might prefer a set or fixed schedule: weekly, monthly or quarterly. Others might choose mutually agreed convenient sessions with mentor/mentee or as career and/or life's experiences demand.

It is a good thing for you and your partner-mentor to determine an agenda that best suits your schedule from time to time as well as feedback preferences. There are times face-to-face meetings do not seem feasible. That is when technology provides options: i.e. telephone, Skype, or acceptable, private methods.

The important caution is to ensure that we are connected and accountable: always willing and ready to learn. Growth and adapting to what we learn do not come easy or suddenly plus the fact that every one's learning capability differs.

Simply stated, it serves no purpose to make mentoring a burden to either party: mentor/mentee.

A point of clarification on the need to have life-long mentoring in our lives though: mentoring does not create an atmosphere of subservience neither does it compel us to a life of patronage. You are not the mentor's customer or client. You are his partner – even though he may know better, be older or more experienced than you.

And even then, a mentor is someone that you should feel comfortable with or building trust could be far-fetched.

Mentoring does not tie us to a particular person life-long if the relationship is not working. We have the option to choose different mentors along the way, as we transition into new careers or locations or even as we consider the mentor's relationship relevant or not to our situation.

In addition, if the chemistry of your mentor is not compatible with yours, or s/he is not making expected contribution to your life or lacks commitment to your partnership, it sure makes sense to have an unwritten exit clause in your relationship, perhaps it is time to move on and look elsewhere.

We need to realize though, that as humans, we all are rather complex beings. It becomes necessary from time to time to give the partnership-mentoring relationship the benefit of maturing before calling it.

"VILLAGE" MENTORING?

In a world that most people live to themselves and under suspicion; where you hardly know your next door neighbor not to talk of relating; where what you do is nobody's business, mentoring becomes increasingly challenging.

It used to be that we were a community and that we assumed our "brother's keeper" in our neighborhood and at Church. Those days seemed gone.

Pastors, like careful neighbors steer away from offending the people, many times because of the fear of being accused as intrusive or losing patronage. But that was not what it used to be.

However, even with declining communal living, due mainly to urban "white collar" migration, still in today's rural environment around the globe, particularly in the third world communities, raising a child continues to take more than the efforts of dad and mom. It is not that the community had formal day-to-day training program, but that certain values are put in place which when observed, serves as default guidance to positive achievements – first and foremost to the village and by implication, to the world around them. Every one contributes to the "unwritten" mentoring program and if anyone tries to deviate from the norm, s/he gets easily brought back – again by realizing that s/he is in a "lone," and "strange" world of his/her choosing. Villagers, relatives and friends alike assure parents that they got their back in the welfare of their ward– which interestingly is all that mentoring is all about: "getting your back."

In a world that most people live to themselves and under suspicion;
where you hardly know your next door neighbor not to talk
of relating; where what you do is nobody's business,
mentoring becomes increasingly challenging.

In those communities, it is not that anyone is really interested in their neighbor's matters considered private and personal; rather, it is that the societies have set values of character that enables members stay out of trouble. It is also that when members are in doubt as to how or what to do in certain situations, someone in the village is available to guide. That is the same concept that the Church ought to exhibit.

It is the pragmatic, supportive, progressive alternative approach: one that builds friendship and the accompanying trust. It motivates the mentee as s/he ploughs through life's predicaments, assuring that s/he is not alone. It builds in the mentee, the spirit of volunteering and the readiness to mentor others as s/he learns the ropes.

Could we change our world by village mentoring concept? You bet.

Yet there have been arguments made on whether or not we actually need "a village to raise a child." I hear words like "too many cooks spoil the broth…" But there could be no better mentoring initiative than that done with discreet and wise counsel of others who have been there and done it.

The Bible is replete with exhortation to village-style mentoring:

> "Plans fail for lack of counsel, but with many advisers they succeed."–Proverbs 15:22 [NIV]

> "Surely you need guidance to wage war, and victory is won through many advisers." - Proverbs 24:6 [NIV]

> "Without wise leadership, a nation falls; there is safety in having many advisers." - Proverbs 11:14 [NLT]

Because it is evident that no single human being has exclusive knowledge, it stands to reason that there will always be safety in multitude of counselors. What one person may have missed may be complimented by another and if it turns out that all agree on one matter, perhaps there is verity and dependability on such issues.

> "…the older men [are] to exercise self-control, to be worthy of respect, and to live wisely. They must have sound faith and be filled with love and patience. Similarly, teach the older women to live in a way that honors God. They must not slander others or be heavy drinkers. Instead, they should teach others what is good. These older

women must train the younger women to love their husbands and their children, to live wisely and be pure, to work in their homes, to do good, and to be submissive to their husbands. Then they will not bring shame on the word of God. In the same way, encourage the young men to live wisely. And you yourself must be an example to them by doing good works of every kind. Let everything you do reflect the integrity and seriousness of your teaching." – Titus 2:2-7 [NLT]

"To the elders among you, I appeal as a fellow elder and a witness of Christ's sufferings who also will share in the glory to be revealed: Be shepherds of God's flock that is under your care, watching over them–not because you must, but because you are willing, as God wants you to be; not pursuing dishonest gain, but eager to serve; not lording it over those entrusted to you, but being examples to the flock. And when the Chief Shepherd appears, you will receive the crown of glory that will never fade away. In the same way, you who are younger, submit yourselves to your elders. All of you, clothe yourselves with humility toward one another, because, "God opposes the proud but shows favor to the humble."   – I Peter 5:1-5 [NIV]

"And let us consider how we may spur one another on toward love and good deeds, not giving up meeting together, as some are in the habit of doing, but encouraging one another–and all the more as you see the Day approaching."
                    – Hebrews 10:24-25 [NIV]

Because it is evident that no single human being has exclusive knowledge, it stands to reason that there will always be safety in multitude of counselors.

DO-NUTS

As good as mentoring is, we could only realize maximum and enduring benefits when we understand and avoid potential pitfalls that most often could render it unrealizable or ineffective:

1. Do not limit who your mentor should be. Provided there is compatibility both by way of chemistry as well as profession, a male with noted integrity could mentor a female mentee and vice versa. Similarly, a white mentor without bias could mentor a mentee of color and the same way around. What's more, someone younger, but who has stayed on the job longer and more experienced could mentor an older, ready-to-learn mentee. It is never a bad idea if in doubt, to ask whether or not your prospective mentor would be inclined to or comfortable with helping you in specific areas of your weakness. If necessary, be open to having more than one mentor. There is something to gain by multitude of counselors.

2. Do not make your mentor play God by setting unrealistic expectations. The dynamics of time, circumstance and mentee's efforts based on capabilities influence deliverables. Mentors are at best guides. They do not or rather should not fix problems. They could only point to the many times when their companions arrive at desired destinations – as testimonials. With the very best of intentions, well laid out trips could easily be cut short or hindered by several uncontrollable factors. So are relationships. Mentors most often ask questions and encourage/direct mentees to find solutions. Setting unrealizable expectations or supposing that the mentor's ideas and recommendations must be all-time sufficient and guaranteed to succeed sets you up for failure. While some level of

optimism is necessary in the mentor-mentee relationship, it does not eliminate vulnerability. The mentoring fun sometimes could be found in the roller-coaster. So be prepared to take a ride and have fun.

3. Do not lose sight of your purpose for mentoring. Allowing too much socializing, chatting, undue familiarity, asking too much time and attention, and involvement in personal affairs could derail the benefits of mentoring. Should mentoring fail to be valuable to the mentee, you have the option to call it, instead of wasting your valuable time. The ability to know where to draw the line at those times that you seem drawn in any of these directions other than desired is what assures strategic progression.

4. Do not publicly disclose details of the mentoring relationship. Remember, as they say: "what happens in Vegas stays in Vegas." Trust is destroyed when the vulnerabilities that you discussed with the mentor in private are publicly disclosed or conversely when what you were told as mentee in confidence becomes subject of discussion among peers. There might be instances when it becomes necessary for a mentor to remind the mentee of a prior pitfall, as a way of avoiding a repeat. This should not be seen as bruising old wounds but received as a gentle admonition.

5. Do not attempt to copy-cat your mentor. It is limiting to want to be exactly like your older mentor. Realize that your mentor is not you neither are you his descendant. A parent could very well serve as mentor, but s/he is usually more of a role model. You cannot and should not attempt to be him/her. Instead, allow your mentor to help guide you through the weak spots. If he has had any as may usually be the case, he might be able to share how he scaled the challenge – for your "now" benefit. Notwithstanding, know that the interplay of time, circumstance and people are not always identical in a mentor-mentee relationship. Worse still, reactions

to life and situations differ. Use the mentor's guide-notes quite alright, but be yourself in execution.

6. Do not dump your mentor when you have succeeded. Recognize and appreciate him/her and the guidance you received. Avoiding or looking down on your mentor when you have succeeded is not only cruel and opportunistic; it has a way of getting back at you around the corner. From time to time, when you receive a guidance that worked for you, respect your mentor by acknowledging his/her effort – no matter how small.

> *Find a mentor because he/she can teach you things you won't find in a book.*

CPSIA information can be obtained
at www.ICGtesting.com
Printed in the USA
FFOW04n1519140116
20431FF

9 781498 454094